An Evening with
JonBenét Ramsey

An Evening with JonBenét Ramsey

Walter A. Davis

Authors Choice Press
New York Lincoln Shanghai

An Evening With JonBenét Ramsey

All Rights Reserved © 2003, 2004 by Walter A. Davis

No part of this book may be reproduced or transmitted in any form or by any means, graphic, electronic, or mechanical, including photocopying, recording, taping, or by any information storage or retrieval system, without the written permission of the publisher.

Authors Choice Press
an imprint of iUniverse, Inc.

For information address:
iUniverse, Inc.
2021 Pine Lake Road, Suite 100
Lincoln, NE 68512
www.iuniverse.com

Originally published by Xlibris

NOTE: This is a work of fiction based on extensive research. Any resemblance to actual persons and events is a function of insight.

ISBN: 0-595-30968-2 (Pbk)
ISBN: 0-595-76468-1 (Cloth)

Printed in the United States of America

CONTENTS

COWBOY'S SWEETHEART 11

THERE IS ANOTHER COURT 107

CASTING THE AUDIENCE: TOWARD
   A THEATRE OF PRIMARY EMOTIONS 159

ENDNOTES TO THERE IS ANOTHER COURT 181

APPENDIX: LEGAL MEMORANDUM ON
   FIRST AMMENDMENT CONCERNS 201

For

JonBenét Ramsey

(August 6, 1990—December 26, 1996)

TRUST PROVISION

I have established a Trust—The Davis Trust for Aid in the Prevention and Treatment of Child Sexual Abuse. All money due me from the sale of *An Evening With JonBenét Ramsey* and from any productions of the play *Cowboy's Sweetheart* will be donated to this Trust. Funds from the Trust will be given to organizations who work on behalf of sexually abused children.

COWBOY'S SWEETHEART

CONTENTS

ACKNOWLEDGMENTS 15
CAST OF CHARACTERS 17
ACT ONE—"DO ROSES KNOW
  THEIR THORNS HURT?" 19
ACT TWO—TO WALK ON SOMETHING ALIVE 47
ACT THREE—THE DOOR TO SUMMER 79
ENDNOTE 103
BIBLIOGRAPHY 105

ACKNOWLEDGMENTS

Thanks to the following friends for advice and support: Margaret Allen, Hannah Berkowitz, Alex Blazer, Ghislaine Boulanger, Marilyn Brownstein, Lonnie Carter, John Champlin, Gretchen Cline, Deb Colvin-Tener, Chris Davis, Connie Davis, Darcy Davis, Lu Davis, Michael Eigen, Amy Finnerty, Leigh Gilmore, Lyle Hammerberg, Gary Heim, Nick Kaldis, Sebastian Knowles, Kara Kostiuk, Jim Kozicki, Victoria List, Gretchen Luidens, Julian Markels, Clarissa Markiewicz, Todd McGowan, Jane Mowder, Hilary Neroni, Dorry Noyes, Elizabeth Patnoe, Tom Perna, Tom Postlewait, Elizabeth Renker, Roseanne Rini, Marjorie Rowe, Devin Schindler, Sue William Silverman, F.L.Simons, Justin Simons, John Tener, Melanie Rae Thon, Devin Willis, and Michael J. Zitta. And a special word of thanks to the cast of the first production of this work, a staged reading that was given in Denney Hall at The Ohio State University on November 27, 2000: Catherine Tosenberger, Emily Leverett, Sharon Mitchell, Eddy Williams, Nick Baldesare, and Steve Ponton.

Two special words of acknowledgment. To Lois Tyson who has lived through all of it with me and who has taught me that love is the ability to let the other be true to inner necessities wherever they lead. To my son, Stephen Davis, actor and director: I'll never forget the golden week we spent in the summer of 2001, from early morning until late every night going over every scene, scanning each line, revising, arguing, creating together. Your insights were invaluable in enabling me to bring the play to its current form. Your creative spirit and your great human generosity are alive in it, part of its very fabric.

CAST OF CHARACTERS

Jolie Brady   at 6, 9,12,15, 35, 30, and 45 years of age
                               [Played in all scenes by the same adult actress]
Mitzi Brady   (Jolie's mother)—age 40 (and 70 in Act III)
Pauline Pratt   (Mitzi's mother)—age 80
Jonathan Lyons Brady (Jolie's father)—age 50 (and 80 in Act III)
Josh Friedrickson   (Professor of Drama at a large University)

ACT ONE—"DO ROSES KNOW THEIR THORNS HURT?"

SET: The stage is divided in half with the upstage portion—hereafter termed the Inner Stage—behind a semi-transparent screen of sheer curtains that are attached to the top of a wooden frame. Actions on this stage can be dimly seen through the curtains, on which words and images can also be projected. The curtains can also be drawn to the side to make this playing space directly visible. The playing space inside the screen is boxed in, creating, in effect, the image of a large television. Lighting can come from behind and from stage Right and Left of the Inner Stage and from its front when action requires projecting shadows on back wall. All lighting should be used to give actions that occur on this Inner Stage an expressionistic quality. To the right and left of the screen are two black doors with black curtains at head level. All this is dark at rise, however, for the action begins on the Outer Stage.

SCENE ONE—OUTER STAGE

RISE: Voices heard in the dark, continuing as spotlight comes up on the face of a woman seated center stage, facing audience.

MITZI'S VOICE

No no no no no no no No. You're getting it all wrong. Again.

From the top. (*Sings following line*) "I want to be a Cowboy's Sweetheart, I—"

PAULINE'S VOICE

Sing out, Jolie, Sing Out! You want to be Miss America someday it begins here missy.

JONATHAN'S VOICE

That's what you are baby, Daddy's Girl.

PAULINE'S VOICE

Oh, law, she carries her body like a sack of wood. Keep going, nobody told you to stop.

JONATHAN'S VOICE

You don't have to tell me it hurts. It has to hurt for a while.

MITZI'S VOICE

Speak up. What have you got to say for yourself. Nothing. Good. Here's what nothing gets you. (*Loud noise of slap.*)

Light now comes up full on the young woman seated center stage. Next to her a side table: on it an ashtray, cigarettes, bottled water, and a glass with ice. She is Jolie Brady, age 35, smartly dressed in a grey business-like suit. Hair short and brushed back. Glasses. The light that rises on her must appear to come directly from the audience and should be played in a way that suggests she is under an increasingly intense spotlight. She reaches for cigarette but before lighting it begins speaking in what will be a series of monologues. All of her monologues move, with great fluidity, in two directions. The fourth wall is broken often as she directly addresses the audience—and often particular individuals in the audience. But there is also, throughout, a frequent movement into a privacy, into the deepest recesses of an inner consciousness in which she speaks only to herself. In a sense the entire play takes place inside her head. It is her living out of that endless conversation we all have with ourselves and with the others inside us who speak to us when we are most alone, whose questions and comments interrupt our thought and whom we address in profoundly contradictory ways whenever we engage the agon that is our inner world. And as she speaks we become that audience—and thus a central protagonist in the ensuing drama. Jolie's struggle to articulate herself to herself and to the audience is the heart of the play and the challenge the monologues pose for the actress who must dramatize the internal conflicts that define them. She has concentrated her being into the desire to understand her experience and she comes to us from that place, burning, "still signaling through the flames." Jolie is the wedding, within the context of psychological realism, of expressionism, theatre of cruelty, and feminist performance art. What else could she be? She was theatre before she could be anything else—formed so by her mother. The media then made her fantastically theatrical, the sop to the voyeurism of a mass audience. She has always been on stage, looked at by an audience. She speaks now, however, with a Brechtian task—to reverse that relationship so that we, not she, are held under the gaze.

JOLIE

I read most of the night. When its cold and dark and silent, that's when its best. Nothing but the little light behind my head and the page, the words. Nothing to distract me.

You see—after—I have to be alone after. That's the kind of thing you want to know about, isn't it? No, I was never without someone—when I wanted. But I always made them leave—after. To be alone and read, with the night like a solitude all about you. I know. I know. It's so trite. When I was emptied out, then words came alive. But it wasn't like that. It's the distractions. They're everywhere. But late at night they fade away. Words too fall away until there's nothing left but this (*tapping forehead, a gesture repeated often throughout monologues*), alone, seeking the single sentence. The one where everything stops. Reading—for me that's always been the most violent act.

Okay, okay I lied. Sometimes they stayed, slept the night. It's too much trouble otherwise. You never know what some guy'll think he's entitled to because you went to bed with him. Well three a.m. scenes aren't my style. Better to be alone together.

Yes you bet goddamn right the reading was often best then. To know I hadn't been touched. Beside me in bliss one of the biologically blessed—a body at peace, dumb to the stirrings of mind. I beside it more awake than ever—in my body, a body alert, alive to its own knowing. (*Brief nervous laugh.*) You bet, give me a good read and I'm your perfect partner for the comedy of the next morning. You know, the one where kindness is the language of evasion. Hell yes a good read and I'll say whatever you gotta hear as complement to your fucking.

(*Holds throat, effort to catch breath before continuing: this action to occur at other times during monologue.*)

I'm sorry. I couldn't breathe there for a minute. Hot black coffee, cigarettes, slow time, a book, and night folded in upon itself. To lie there like that and come upon a sentence that bites into you like a judgment—that's what reading is.

Yes sometimes yes when I found nothing but words then yes it all gave way to nights of a different kind, when the whole thing circled in on itself, in a vertigo, only I was falling in words, out of myself, away from myself, reading the trap I threw myself into with renewed effort page after empty page. And I remember, it was one of those times when there was nothing but what you call anxiety. When anxiety drew a curtain between me and the world. I'd wake in a panic. Consciousness was nothing but images flashing, voices, feelings broken loose inside me. And the craziest thing, with all this going on *I functioned*. I went to work and had long conversations in which I didn't hear a single word, afraid that any moment it would all tumble out and the only thing left when they came to get me a weeping I could no longer contain. That's how I lived—for months—in a general insurrection that could only end with one thing: the extinction of *this* (*taps forehead*).

You talk about a death-drive. Death for me was then a pressure in the nerves. And something else—finally—an uncanny pleasure. "They don't see it," I said, "any of it. I can go on like this, indefinitely. "The whole arrangement—what you call the world—it requires so slight an investment. Master a few moves-words-gestures and you're free. All the time. For this (*taps forehead*). For what beats here. Every waking moment can be given to it. No need to stop. Nothing out there to get in the way.

That's how far I'd gone—that time. Only one thing held me back. Every day, after work, I'd go to the University Library, to the stacks where they keep the psych books. I'd walk among them, touch them, whisper the titles. "One. One holds the key. Tonight." Because there was a wager here too, a pact. I could take only one book. Each day. And I had to read it—all of it—that night.

That's how I found it. My sentence, the one that brought me here, made me want to come here. I don't remember the name of the book—a collection of essays by an analyst named Bion. I'm a lousy scholar. No time, order so what I do is I write down sentences—the ones I wait for when I read—on scraps of paper. I keep them with me here.
 (*Opens purse and takes out a few from among many crumpled pages. She holds these pages gently, touching them with love, opening one with care, which she then reads.*)

"*Inquiry begins when love is doubted.*" Some sentences Christ you read them and know your life will never be the same. That someone could know that, write a sentence like that. That others, shrinks, could come together in little rooms dedicated to the violence of it. That some day, maybe I . . . The book fell away. Something broke inside me.

I remember everything about that night. The acrid smell of the room, the slant of light, the heft of it, the book, the chill in my fingers, and the hot feeling here (*indicating chest*) as I lay there with my eyes shut so I could see the words detach themselves and hang above me, the letters like stencils carved in the ceiling. I lay there like that, in a hush, as dark turned to dawn and it was only when I felt the light on my eyelids that I realized I was crying, the tears warm and slow down my face. And I held myself then, because then I was afraid I couldn't stop. "They'll find me like this, here . . . beyond reclaiming." And so I rocked myself and wrestled it down. But I remember—I'll never forget it—my face in the mirror when I was finally able to get up. You know how sometimes you catch your face—your real face—when you've forgotten to compose it before you look. My face: it was all on fire. My eyes—they're green—but then they were like emeralds. The points of my hair—where it rats out in the night—were all ablaze with sparks of light. And my mouth, it was open in an O, with my hand holding it, like this, almost caressing it.

Then, before the mirror, (*shifting into Mitzi's voice*) "Makeup first, Jolie, before anything else. Get your face on"—it faded. My face faded. But I could see it still receding. And then the hot tears broke in me again and I felt it—Joy in me—that I'd found it, finally, something I could love. Something I want. (*Long Pause*)

Do you have any idea how terrifying it is for me to want anything?

(BLACKOUT)

SCENE TWO—INNER STAGE

RISE: The year 1996 flashes on screen of Inner Stage which then parts as bright lights rise on this stage. Outer Stage remains in darkness during all scenes that take place on inner stage.

MITZI
NO. No no no no no no no no. You're getting it all wrong. Again. From the top.

PAULINE
(*To Mitzi*) Ohh, law. It's a mess. She can't just flop around like that. (*To Jolie*) That's right, young lady. This is for your ears too. Well, don't just stand there. Time's wasting. Practice your steps. Your poses.

MITZI
Entertain em, JuJuBee. Like this.
  (*Mitzi here goes into the "Cowboy's Sweetheart" number and plays it fulsome, seductively.*)

"I want to be a Cowboy's Sweetheart/ I want to learn to rope and to ride . . ." Now, a one, a two—

JOLIE
(*Halting, in attempt to mimic Mitzi*) "I want to be a Cowboy's Sweetheart/ I want to learn to rope—"
  (*Jolie in all scenes on inner stage should be played by the same actress who plays the adult Jolie. All scenes involving the young Jolie thus take on a Brechtian function: the audience sees an adult woman playing a child who is trying to act like a sexualized adult woman. **Under no circumstances should a child be cast in any production of this work.***)

PAULINE
Sing out, Jolie, sing out.

MITZI
That's it, baby, now sell it. Sell it

PAULINE
She couldn't sell lemonade in a heat wave. (*Jolie haults, confused.*)

(*To Jolie*) Keep going. Nobody told you to stop. Just like you, Mitzi. No attention span.

MITZI

I've got an idea, JuJuBee. Let's see if we can get the pose right first.
> (*She here positions Jolie in that pose that beauty queens love: the head turned back over the shoulder looking down invitingly at the stuck out derriere. Mitzi then acts out what follows, to illustrate.*)

Hold the pose. Yes, nose turned up like that. Then, you flick your hair as you turn your head away. Like this. Now, watch: you sash-shay around in a half-circle. The hand stays on the hip, elbow pointed out. Then halfway through the turn you give them what they've been waiting for—that SMILE. Time that smile just right, baby, and they'll be eating out of your hands. That's how you grab an audience. Okay, you try. No. From where you take the pose.
> (*Jolie now tries to mimic Mitzi but rushes it, gets confused, stops abruptly.*)

PAULINE

Oh Law, she carries her body like a sack of wood. A Southern Lady has breeding, manners. She is a thing of culture, rich in traditions passed on from generation to generation. (*Sees Jolie is not listening. Shouts.*) This is for you, Jolie. True beauty is not a transitory thing, a thing of fashion. It comes from within—

MITZI

—Oh, mother, Pull-leez.

PAULINE

Well you better find some way to get through to her or she'll make a fool of you come Spring. Get her some high level instruction, that's my advice.

MITZI
(*Turns to child, speaking in voice like Pauline's*) Don't just stand there slumped over like that. Try it again. "I want to be a cowboy's sweetheart." Listen to the rhythm of the words. That tells your body what to do. "I WANT TO BE A COWBOY'S SWEETHEART."
   (*Jolie tries again and momentarily creates something that is spontaneous, innocent, but also furtive, broken from within by the anticipation of their criticisms.*)

PAULINE
No, for the love of sweet jesus don't be going off on your own like that. Follow the directions we gave you.

JOLIE
(*Makes ugly facial gesture, then mutters under her breath.*) Yes, Grandma Pratt . . .

MITZI
(*Loud clap of hands.*) Don't you get snippy with your Grandma Pratt, young lady. Apologize! This instant!

PAULINE
Listen up. You're going to do this until you get it right.

There'll be no excuses in this family, missy. You want to be Miss America someday it begins here.

JOLIE
No. No more. Not til Daddy gets home.

PAULINE
If we tell you to do it you'll do it.

MITZI
(*Aside to Pauline, then smarmy to Jolie*) Hold on, mom. I've got

an idea. Baby, I bet if we try real hard we can have it perfect by the time Daddy gets home. Wouldn't that be great? For your Daddy. A perfect performance. You want to make your Daddy proud, don't you?

JOLIE

But, Mommy, it's so hard. I try and—

MITZI

—A contract to try is a contract to fail. Don't try. Do it. You're close, baby. I can feel it. Trust me. Remember, "Wherever you go/ whatever you do/ We're gonna go through it TOGETHER . . .

(*Mitzi here goes into what she calls their song, "Together" from Gypsy. Sings it sappy while hectoring Jolie with gestures until Jolie reluctantly joins in. Briefly they sing it together.*)

PAULINE

It's hopeless, Mitzi. Maybe she should just go off to her room and think about getting things right the next time.

MITZI

Not yet, mom. She's close. I can feel it. JuJuBee, remember what I showed you before? How at the end you stand there with your hand on your hip? Yes, like that. Now pay attention. What are you feeling, right now—inside? That's the key. Keep that feeling when you move and it'll come.

(*To Mitzi's prompting, Jolie starts again, now mimicking Mitzi's provocative gestures. At some point in what follows Jonathan enters from the side—a shadow projected onto the stage—and watches, undetected.*)

Yes, like that. Make them want more. Yes, charm them with your eyes. That little pout I showed you. Now, give the skirt a twirl as you turn then come right back at them, right to the edge of the stage. Like Miss America. Then turn, turn and walk

away—almost like you're dismissing them. But then you stop. You turn the head back over your shoulder. Yes, yes, hold that pose. Make them want it. Now, wrap them in your arms.
(*Jolie now made anxious, troubled by her own gestures, by what is being prematurely solicited in her so that when she stops she is near tears.*)

Ask me that's a lot closer. She's come alive.

PAULINE
I suppose. But something's still missing. I'll bet every one of them can move like that. It's still too cutsey. In the feather costume it'll all look foolish if all the poses and turns aren't letter perfect.

MITZI
Okay, mother, okay. She's not going to get it all tonight. A good night's sleep, that's what we all could use. How's that sound to you, JuJuBee, a good sleep and a fresh start in the morning?

JOLIE
But you promised. When Daddy gets home. I get to do it for him.

MITZI
I said to bed.

JOLIE
It's not fair. You promised.

MITZI
Those are marching orders, young lady. And don't forget what we do before lights out. That's right, the diaper. You know what happens when you forget. And with you soiling all the time too now. Disgusting.

(Jolie stands broken, in tears, unable to move.)

And get all that makeup off too. Linda said she can't get the stains out of the pillow case.
(Jolie does not move.)

I said Go. You know where.
(Jolie runs from stage, crying.)

(BLACKOUT)

SCENE THREE—INNER STAGE

RISE: Screen parted. The child in her bedroom before mirror removing makeup. This action continues throughout the scene. Sits directly facing audience. Scene bathed in a soft light. At rise looking at herself in mirror. Stops. Takes up Teddy Bear. Holds it gently.

JOLIE

Just you and me Brownie. You and me . . . *(Mimicking Mitzi and Pauline)* "Apologize to your Grandma Pratt, JuJuBee." "A lady doesn't walk like that . . . a lady."
(Pause. Then makes her eyes look Asian and plays with that look as she remembers recently seen video of Nancy Kwan in **Flower Drum Song**.*)*

Look, Brownie, what I can do. See. My eyes. Like the girl in the movie. She danced around the room singing. Not like they want. But like Nala, when she walks. Nala.

Yes. I know. Get it all off like Mommy said. I try. But I can't. And it's all muss now. A spot here. Another. And I don't like this face now. It's like the one mommy makes when she—
(Long pause. Freezes in frightened look.)

It's only good when I get it clean again and smooth. With the cream. Then it's like sleep. Like the roses. They don't know their thorns hurt. They can't . . . when we touch them, their fingers so small, folding in each one, like sleep . . .

But not tonight Brownie tonight we got to stay awake. For Daddy. To tell him. What I saw today. *The Lion King.* But not like in a cartoon. But people. Alive. Like me. All dressed up with big masks. On a stage like me. The animals alive in the people. So when they move, they're the animals, the people. They sway back and forth like fields of flowers then leap and dance and stomp the ground. All together. In a big circle. Simba and Nala and even Scar, the lady lions and the big dancing birds. Dancing. Like I told auntie Pam at the beach, when she made me put the shoes on. "No, I want to feel it, the life of the earth under my feet." Like Nala when they wrestle and she flips Simba then they laugh and arch their necks together. Like this Brownie. She's brave, too, Nala. She's not afraid of Scar. The hyenas can't scare her. She goes right into the desert all alone and gets the lady lions to fight for Simba. She could split Scar in two. Cause she's not afraid. Nothing can—

(*Full stop. Dissolves briefly in sobs which she tries to smother. Now shifts to her nightly duty, to putting on the Diaper trainer pants she has been ordered to wear, knowing that she will wet and probably also soil herself again this night.*)

I know, Brownie. That's why I put them on now. So I won't worry when the dreams come and Mommy takes me to the cold room where the light stabs at me with her face all twisted up like Scar and her voice that pulls me around and hisses at me what I am.
(*During this in involuntary memory her face pulled back and around like a horse reined back with bit in mouth.*)

If he'd only come Brownie. Daddy. I'm afraid. Afraid I'll fall asleep. But there's a trick. I know it. See. Cause when I wet my finger and rub my eyes. See, the water; it keeps them open. Then I can lie quiet and wait cause when I'm quiet, that's when

Daddy comes. Daddy. And I know he'll take us when I ask him. Far away we'll fly and I bet he gets us a seat right up front so we can see it, like in the picture I saw, all in a big circle with the Lion King on top of the Mountain looking down so strong and Sarabi the beautiful lady lion with the white mane moving down the mountain . . . so slow . . . so you can see it . . . when she moves . . . the earth alive in her feet . . . it comes up into her body, like waves moving across her back . . . the earth moving in her, down the long path . . . to them . . . to Simba and Nala, where they wait.

(*The scene now slowly fades to black, with her curled, still rubbing moisture in her eyes ever more slowly as she drifts into sleep.*)

(BLACKOUT)

SCENE FOUR—OUTER STAGE

RISE: Monologue of adult Jolie resumes. Seated as before, facing audience. Rest of outer stage is now empty.

JOLIE

I wore my face at school one day. Eighth grade. Mitzi'd transferred me to a Catholic school. Gotten it into her head the nuns were the finishing touch I needed. Eighth grade. Remember: when every boy at his desk rides a hard-on and every girl fidgets in a confused anticipation.

Morning recess. I hide in a stall then sit before the mirror. I rat my hair then pencil the eyebrows so they slant—like this— then darken them all around with eye shadow and color my lips the richest red and full. Last I hollow the cheeks. This is the hardest part, to get it just right, the shadows that give it that hungry look they love. I already had my costume on. All I had to do was pull the skirt a little higher over the belt and tighten it. For myself alone: I'd worn the garter belt and now I put on the nylons and draw them up slow, waiting for that moment when I feel them together: nylon ends cool, flesh begins warm. I linger touching my inner thighs. Then smooth down the skirt and sit. Like this. Until I'm ready.

Back in class no one notices. I walk to my desk with my head down, my fingers scratching at my scalp, and bury my face in a book. Only when I'm ready, then I look up. At Sister Inez. She gives no sign at first, just a blank look like something interrupted her train of thought for a moment but now she's flicked it off, the way you brush off a mosquito. I almost cry then, then I see the change. The blank look was just shock, cause now she gets that tight smile in the lips and that fixed look in the eyes that comes whenever she lectures us on her subjects—and you'll like this—about nuns being Christ's bride, the body a "temple of the holy ghost," Saint Juliana "virgin and martyr" and the others embracing death to save their virtue. The eyes are slits—boring into me. The fingers snap, summoning me forward. We stand before them, facing each other. I wait for the slap I can already feel sharp and hot on my face. I wait proud but it doesn't come. "Face the class," she commands, turning me around at the shoulders. A hush. No one moves. I can see it in their faces. They're spellbound. The whole year has been building toward this and they know it.

Her voice, I hear it still, rising in pitch, almost remember them exactly, the words. "This. See what I mean. Can't wait, can you, to be like this?" Then, to me. "Think you could fool me. Think I don't know you've been riding around in cars with high school boys. Puffing yourself up so big. But that you'd dare to flaunt it here." She stopped, paused. I don't know what she expected. Tears. Some broken plea. A struggle to escape. Cause I could feel it now, her fingers pressing down here (*touches collarbone and neck*) turning me back to her. I got to hand it to her though, she had a real sense of theatre. It was like she was positioning me so I wouldn't upstage myself, so we'd be face to face in profile before them. But there was still pride in me then and something else. This was the moment I'd been waiting for too. So I held my pose and milked the pause. Then I did it. Slow, deliberate, defiant and free—I smiled. I looked her right in the eyes—and smiled.

And there was something different in them too now, something I'd never see before. A panic, like an animal caught in the headlights of a car at night. Then outrage. I could see it, a shaking in her hands and then I felt it, the fingers at my cheeks (*Jolie here holds fingers forward toward audience and mimics cat claw scratch during following line*) then sharp and deep as they raked down the length of my face and with it a sound, a keening at first then a long howl like a fire-engine across the night.

You know how a cat-scratch at first all you see is the long thin line of the cut, clear, abrupt, and clean. Then how little spots of blood pop up, isolated, before they come together and flow. That's what it must have been like to them. There was a long still moment, lifted out of time and held there pure so they could look at me, at the long lines cut down my face. Then it all ran together and I saw it too, the blood in drops hitting the wooden floor. No one moved. None of those boys—who brayed all the time about how tough they were, their pants chafing, whimpered a single word. Not even when I started to shake all over.

(BLACKOUT)

SCENE FIVE—INNER STAGE

RISE: Curtain screen parted. In the dark a man's cry, a piercing howl of pain, followed by choked sobs. Lights come up on Jonathan Lyons Brady, awakened from sleep by his own cry, now pacing the room in the night. Mitzi in the bed sleeps on.

JONATHAN

My little girl. I don't know what's happening to your Daddy, baby. I can't get it to stop. I'm scared, baby. Your Daddy is scared. Oh Ruth, my darling one, I miss you so. My little girl. Only 18 and gone. Brutal. Random. Insane. A truck and a car crash on an icy road and my dream for you, your beautiful life, taken from me. Forever. Nothing left, nothing but this hole. (*Jabs at chest with index finger.*) Loss, like a hole in the center of the world and christ baby I'm scared. Cause it's in the dream now. I keep reaching out to touch your face, your beautiful face. But I'm inside the hole now. I push the arm out, the hand opens, the fingers strain to touch you but then you're thrown back in endless space and I wake again with this fucking weeping that won't stop.

(*Moves to table. Takes up Ruth's picture and 5x7 card attached to it—his "poem." Struggling to find the right words. Stops often, dissatisfied with his poetic efforts.*)

If I could find the words. A poem, to you . . ."Cause the best part of every day/ When you get to be with daddy's girl . . . For in my heart you reign so dear /However long or brief the year/ Beside me to take away a tear./ And you are starting to have woman's looks which are now clear—

(*Stops. Searches for next line. Mumbling.*)

A looks . . . tear, drear . . .

(*Goes back. Silently rereads certain lines. Rising frustration. In defeat drops the paper on the desk. Sobbing begins again. Rises. Paces again. To Blackout. In it sobbing, but diminished. Then long silence. When light comes back up he is at Jolie's bedside, turning on night-light beside sleeping child. Sits on bed beside her. Looking at her his sobbing begins again. She wakes. Bursts with joy when she sees him.*)

JOLIE

You're Home. Oh Daddy you came. I knew you would. And

ohhh I'm sorry daddy I tried really to stay up for you, to show you . . . What's wrong, Daddy. Why are you crying? I did my best Daddy. I tried. And Mommy said, she promised—

JONATHAN
Shuh. Shuh. Baby it's allright, you didn't do anything wrong. It's here, baby. (*Touching chest*) Here. I'm so scared. I don't know what's happening to your daddy, baby. I can't get it to stop.

JOLIE
Oh, but daddy, please, please don't cry. I know something, daddy. It will make you happy. It's a surprise. Remember *The Lion King*? I saw it today on TV Daddy. But it's real now, with live people up on a stage—like me. They're so big. The Lion King and Scar and the hyenas. They crouch down like a ball and then they jump out, like colors exploding, ohhh and Nala, Daddy, if you could only see her, Nala.

JONATHAN
—You love your daddy don't you, baby? And you know, don't you, how lonely I'd be without you?

JOLIE
But I'm here daddy. I'll never leave you.

JONATHAN
Oh baby if it were only true. If I ever lost you.
    (*Rises from bed. Paces. What follows to be played as an aside, as the memory of Ruth returns and with it a rage.*)

Christ, if I could only sleep. But no. Every night, the same. On and on. I've got to find a way to stop it, don't you understand ? Can't you see that? Every night, the same. Every night, like a dagger—here . . .
    (*Pause. Trying to calm himself. Turns back to Jolie. Sits again on side of bed. She reaches out to him.*)

JOLIE
Not now daddy please. Here. Here, let me. (*She here wipes away his tears.*) That's better, isn't it?
(*She touches his face, then hugs him, holds him, tries to soothe him.*)

JONATHAN
Yes. Like this. Lay back now, baby. That's good. Yes. Just lay there like that so I can look at you.

(BLACKOUT)

SCENE SIX—OUTER STAGE

RISE: As before. Adult Jolie, seated, facing audience.

JOLIE
Ah, the poor thing, you'll say, never to have known anything different. Never to have known love when it's innocent and tender, when trust leads two down each tentative step as their bodies bloom together. That's where you're wrong. There was a boy. Once. He was different. It was different with him. Like an island with him. The first time we talked, at a school picnic, the thing I'll never forget, that I'll always treasure, he acted like there was nothing different about me. We sat together under a great elm and just talked, that golden afternoon, about books, music, our plans for college and the great leap toward freedom that haloed that word. And I remember that night lying awake in bed—after—thinking how easy it would be to slide into your world, to Lethe myself on the lotus of his tenderness. Because he was gentle. He tried to be gentle. There was nothing unkind about him. I could see that, even if he couldn't. Men can't you know, especially when they're young. There was a tenderness in the way he was with me. Everything was slow like a warm bath easing me into him and so when we finally made love it was . . . it felt to me, like the first time. I trusted

him—the way trust is when something in you goes out into another person, something you can never call back. Yes, I loved . . . loved him. And so I told him, as much as I could, about Mitzi and Jonathan . . . No, he didn't. He held me and I was even able to cry for a while . . . No, no nothing was different at first. I'm sorry, that's not true. I could feel it then already, something different in the way he touched me. The tenderness had turned into a kind of sadness. When he touched me now it was like he was witnessing, testifying to some generalized sympathy for life's victims. My body had become something about himself he needed to prove as much as the other boys had to prove how cruel they could be. No of course there was no way I could get him to talk about it. We were kids. Briefly, in our confusion, we made a haven that turned into a prison. For me, for me it was like his fingers were choking me—inside—cutting off everything in here (*here moves hands down body from breast to womb*) that could breathe and flow outward toward him. Then it got so I wanted to run screaming or rake my hands across his face: "fuck me for christsake, here like this let me get on top and ride myself down into you." That's how it ended. I protected him from himself. His hand never took back from my flesh the change in it. He felt what he needed to feel. I felt his need free me back into mine.

(BLACKOUT)

SCENE SEVEN—INNER STAGE

RISE: The curtain screen is drawn across the playing space. Lights up sharp, penetrating on Mitzi's face. She moves almost like a sleepwalker, her lines those of an inner monologue from the depths of her unconscious psyche. The light in this scene comes from the flashlight she holds in her hands. Light throughout scene played expressionistically, jolting, fragmented, in keeping with the psychotic unraveling enacted in the scene.

MITZI

If I do it quick while she lays there like sleep. No sound. Nothing from her. Little bitch smiling at me like that all through dinner. Think you can fool me after what I've been through. Cancer. Stage 4 Ovarian Cancer. That's what they said. You've got cancer, Mitzi, the worst kind. But I knew, even then, after they cut me stem to stern, I knew you'd make me a miracle Lord, praise Jesus, my body healed through Thy Word like a great pageant sweeping down the aisle in Atlantic City, the soul cleansed, every touch burned away, Thy face through dark glass in the chemo—a thousand points of light radiated into my womb.

But now it shatters like a mirror exploding inside me, stabbing me here with unkindness . . . like the spangles from that little slut's costume, leaping from her into me . . . the heart like gall now, each bitter taste. That sow fart laughing at me again. "Got yourself a rich one all right, honeychild. Remember, Jonathan's job is to make the money, ours to spend it." Rich one—poking at me every night. And now that mewling, every night. Expect me to wake for that? open myself to that? but it takes everything not to laugh to hear him knit and unknit his poem every night, his dead letter—to Her. Not to you little bitch, think you're anything but a copy—of me! Fuck you up down and sideways he'll never find his precious Ruth in you. Me. I'm the one who dressed you and taught you how to prance about and twirl your little pussy in his face. And something else you and Ruth will never know. It's me he's after. Me he wishes he could still get it off of.

But the cancer made me free, ate up all the poisons from their ruttings. What you'll learn soon enough little bitch. Momma was right about one thing. It's best when you learn how to beat them off nice and quick into a handkerchief and you're done cause then you get to watch the moron look they get on their faces when they cum. See that a few times it makes you free.

(*Large shadows on back wall rise up then quickly disappear from this point on throughout remainder of scene.*)

But down. They keep pulling me down. I raised myself up—so high. And then they pull me down . . . down where its fetid and dank, like mud-leaves in a gutter with it's sex stink.I can make it so tight down there. But then they're poking at me again. Shoving me in a corner, "*momma*" (*this word said here and below as a cry for help in a child's voice*) "*why?*" (*Now in Pauline's voice*) "Why grow a brain with that thing honeychild it'll gobble up the world." The cock like a battering ram pounding at me until I make it tight again, so I can move again, high above them down the aisle, serene above their hungry eyes like mouths gaping until they tear at me again— *the two of them*—grinning like that, laughing at me, bringing it back, all of it: the fumbling in the back seats of cars— "*momma*"—panties ripped in haste, legs splayed across your dashboards . . . . momma down there scratching, clawing at me. "*Daddy, please.*" . . . my cry like a dead letter hurled at your face frozen behind its newspaper . . . . Smiling? I loved you so.

Down in the coal bin where I went to hide from momma he was there the man I saw in the bathroom, lying on the tiles, vomiting worms. Here's down here now, staring at me, the worms all white crawling out from where his hand is moving. I lay in the coal-bin and made myself still. I didn't move even when the rats came crawling across me, chewing at me, slithering pieces of me up and down the drain pipe, dancing in the moonlight, carrying pieces of me to momma where she waits—

(*Mitzi has now reached the bed of her sleeping daughter. The night-light at bedside is on. Mitzi shakes Jolie awake. Jolie sits bolt upright, knowing what comes next.*)

Put out the light. Go. You know where. Go and wait.

(BLACKOUT)

SCENE EIGHT—OUTER STAGE

RISE: Adult Jolie as before, seated center stage, facing audience.

JOLIE

The mind is a razor—it cuts sharp and deep and final. There is a world within the world. Mind ripens there, feeding on touch. The only language is touch: and touch betrays us—into what we dare not know and can't forget. But *you* don't want to hear about that, do you? You want the affairs—my "sex-history" as you call it. A quick rut through college and its humiliations. Then the grand tour—my adventures with the country club set, an adultery or two thrown in to whet your appetite for the image you long for—don't you?—me pinioned on the deck of some yacht, writhing backward, part of the new crop of international whores. Or, better, this: a last look at the bloated suicided body, the face pasty and colorless, as they wheel me out to final curtain.

(*She stops abruptly, confused. Eyes dart about as if she doesn't know where she is. Holds throat. Struggle for breath. Then begins again. Moves skirt up slightly above knee in what follows.*)

Or what if I show them to you, the cuts here (*indicating arms*) and here (*inside shoulder, just above breast*) or if I slide the skirt to the thigh so you can see it, a savage hieroglyphic, written on the body, the fine scars a razor carves into flesh to memorize an impossible awareness. That's what you want, isn't it? To hear how we cut ourselves? How it takes a world of wounds to seal over what bleeds here (*tapping forehead*) yet must remain unspoken? That's what you want, isn't it? Victims, silent, in a long queue, Coriolanus'd, a pageant competing for the milk of human kindness you can't wait to offer as long as we come to you empty and broken.

(*Smoothes down skirt.*)

Sorry. I have none. (*Tapping forehead*) For me it all goes here. Here that the real cuts are made.

I'm sorry. I know this isn't what you want. It can't be. You want to know about love. What we learn from our experiences—even the worst. That's right, isn't it? Okay, but what if I told you I learned how little there is to learn and how far we'll go to deny that knowledge. About all the times I told myself—like you?—"this, this will be different, he won't be like the others . . ." only to say soon "this . . . now I will have done this . . . seen through this . . . now I won't be dupe to this anymore— . . ."

You see I've been on stage since I was four and learned early about roles and audiences, how perfectly suited they are to each other. So it didn't take me long to learn that to fall in love there's only one condition that must be met—but it's an absolute one. You've got to find someone whose disorder matches yours. That's love—perfect symmetry. (*Snaps fingers.*) CLICK.

(*At the snap of her fingers she points to the now visible curtain screen of the inner stage. She steps to its side and delivers what follows as if she is giving an imaginary lecture complete with slides that are projected on a screen behind her. The screen, however, remains blank.*)

Click. The narcissist aloof in his superiority. You know them, ladies, the silent ones, whose recognition is sought but never gained. What a challenge. He's never found that one special woman who'll give him the courage to express his feelings. There must be treasures buried there, waiting to bloom at the touch of a woman's love. What a victory: to be the one he opens himself to. To be there the day it all blossoms in the full flower of its emptiness.

Not to your taste? How's this? Click. The romantic, drunk with the need to draw you into the whirl of his self-destruction. What drama—to be the latest in the long line of the seduced and abandoned. Centerstage at last, free to play the hysteric to his exits and entrances, then savor with the gals the delights of your abjection.

Or this? Click. The man we start to talk about in our thirties—don't we ladies?—the kind, tender, sensitive men. They're out there waiting, longing—for you. For someone just like you. A real woman. Different from all the others. And now that you've finally found each other you can wash away all the bad experiences. Cause you're ready to learn what real acting is: to discover the little murders he must enact daily to hide his failure to be the kind of man he secretly admires. The one who gets to fuck the bad girl. Who you must never be—remember that's all in the past, ladies. Your role, and damn right you better play it to perfection in the sack, the good girl whose job is to keep his little allegory of love insulated from experience.

Click. Click. Click. I was catholic in my loving. I visited all the nostalgias. These just a few hits from my catalogue aria—of a life lived among shadows. Love: the extent to which we'll go to convince ourselves that we exist. That in our romantic life we're creatures of passion and not puppets aping pre-determined roles in comedies we repeat incessantly—as if all of this had anything to do with love.

(BLACKOUT)

SCENE NINE—INNER STAGE

RISE: Curtain screen drawn across the stage. Late night. Basement in Brady house. The entire scene is done in voice-over to shadows projected expressionistically on the back wall. Mitzi's shadow large, looming; Jolie's small, that of a six year old child.

MITZI

Just what do you think you're up to young lady?

JOLIE

(*Remains silent.*)

MITZI

Think I don't know what's going on?

JOLIE

(*Remains silent.*)

MITZI

Don't give me that innocent look. You know what I'm talking about, miss smarty pants?

JOLIE

(*Remains silent.*)

MITZI

Speak up. What have you got to say for yourself?

JOLIE

(*Remains silent.*)

MITZI

Nothing. Good. Here's what nothing gets you. (*Slaps her once, sharp, loud.*)

JOLIE

(*Remains silent, motionless.*)

MITZI

Go. Pick up the cord. (*Jolie complies*) Bring it. Kneel.
   (*Mitzi starts to tie cord around an object she holds in her hand.*)

JOLIE

(*In tears*) I don't care what you do anymore. It doesn't matter. He loves me, not you. And I can stop it, the crying. You can't. (*Pause.*) I can. Because he loves me.
  (*Shadows projected on back wall of a giant form looming over a cowering child. The child's head is drawn back by a cord looped around the neck. In the other hand, aloft, the giant form brandishes an object shaped like a flashlight. Just as the blow from this object is about to descend on the child the scene ends in frozen tableau. In one sense, the entire play takes place in this moment, the last moment of consciousness in which the whole force of the child's being is concentrated, projected into the future, in a clairvoyant and burning awareness.*)

(BLACKOUT)

ACT TWO—TO WALK ON SOMETHING ALIVE

SCENE ONE—OUTER STAGE

RISE: As in Act One. Jolie, seated center stage, speaking directly to audience. First part in a dream like state.

JOLIE

A wolf caught in a trap will gnaw off its own leg in order to be free. They travel the greatest distances—alone, in a world of ice and snow, then kill, at the throat, in a necessity free of pity. You can never tame them. Sometimes they will come close and look at us but every motion is always approach and backing away. The paws poised above the earth tentative, already redolent with withdrawal; the limbs on guard, flexed, but never in flight—in freedom free. And when you look in their eyes you know it—that what they see they never forget. Their eyes look straight through us. And what they see becomes a ruthless will: to raise one's voice in the torchlight of dusk and dawn, to summon, if only oneself, for the insistent plunge beyond all why and what for.

You want to talk about love? Okay. Love, like a knife, rends the curtain. The roles collapse. The stage is bare. The words empty. The only language is touch and touch betrays us—

Something happened to me before I could develop what you call defenses and so I live a sort of peril in a world defined by touch. The screen of indifference you interpose between yourself and the world—you know, that contact barrier that gets you through the day. I've never been able to build one. You inhabit the world. I live in the world within the world—a world where everything is touching and where touch never lies.

(BLACKOUT)

SCENE TWO—INNER STAGE

RISE: As light rises on inner stage the date 1999 appears on the curtain screen. Jolie rises and walks through the curtain screen to her bed and lies down. Blackout. Light rises again as Jonathan enters, walks to bedside, turns on night-light. Jolie, now 9 years old, is awake, lying motionless, propped up by pillows, staring at the ceiling. Jonathan sits on bed. His back screens her body from view. But we still see her face.

JONATHAN
Baby, I thought you'd be asleep.

JOLIE
No . . . . I was . . . but—

JONATHAN
—I'm here now, baby. You couldn't sleep? Me too. It'll be all right. Lay back. Yes, like that. Do you want me to tell you a story?
  (No response from her. He reaches out and touches her forehead, gently)

So cool. I missed you baby. You're so beautiful like this. Your skin so smooth. Like alabaster. No, don't sit up. Close your eyes. Like a dream, baby; like you're dreaming. Like you're a dream and I . . . I can look at you like this, like sleep. Let me tell you how you are to me. How all the sadness . . . everything wrong drifts away, how . . . (*Stops abruptly.*) Why are you turning like that, I told you to hold still?

JOLIE

I'm sorry. It's cold. I feel like . . . you know like it gets when I start to shake like that all over.

JONATHAN

That's because you won't let yourself relax. (*Touching her*) Here, breathe slow. Then everything will be all right. Just for a little while, like this. Just til Daddy's not sad anymore. (*Pause.*) No. Don't freeze up like that. Just relax and breathe, like I told you.

JOLIE

Okay, daddy, okay. Don't be angry. Please. It's getting quiet now, daddy. I'll be allright. It'll . . . I just—

JONATHAN

—I know baby. I can feel it. The best part of every day. When you get to be Daddy's girl. And that's who you are now, baby, daddy's girl.

(BLACKOUT)

SCENE THREE—OUTER STAGE

RISE: Adult Jolie as before, facing audience.

JOLIE

Touch . . . You see a dog chained, all fang, leaping forth and torn back, at the neck, then leaping again in renewed fury to attack what is always behind it, at its throat, wrenching it back, the noose tightening. You see it—as I saw it yesterday on TV at the start of a commercial for—for god knows what. You see it and you feel— what? Fear? Pity? Or the brief stirring between your legs of an insatiable cruelty? You see . . . feel . . . you may even form a concept, a fleeting protest. Then the whole thing dies within you and you move on. I see nothing. A suffering erupts in me and I have no way to stop it. That dog's violation and its dumb terror becomes mine. It enters me and rushes down to join with all the other images waiting to receive it—here (*indicating womb*)—in the place where touch never dies.

(*During what follows the Lights come up in the house so that the audience members become aware of one another.*)

Men, the long line, saying you love me while your hand at my breast is like fingers at my throat draining life from me. Your hand, it speaks your fear, your loathing, your need to take possession of a trophy or coerce a testimony to deny something about yourself you know is true. Touch: all the ways we ooze betrayal. Touch: what the body knows and must sustain—or die. The way you touch me tells me everything: what I am for you . . . who you are . . . everything we invent words in a vain effort to conceal. Touch knows. It is the future in the instant.

My body's the seismograph of your self-deceit. And you wanna know something, fellas, it's not really a subtle science. To know when your tongue in my mouth is like a bullet in my brain. When your dick is a weapon and how you loved it when I was tight and dry, "like a virgin," submitted to the conqueror's right, my cry—of pain goddammit—what gets you off. Or when your mouth smells and pecks at me in the brief affirmation of my sex—oh yeh you guys love to eat pussy allright—the prelude, I feel it already, my head forced down so I can suck long on my self-abasement. Or your eyes, invading me, spying me out, waiting for it, my face abandoned to you in that look you love (*she here mimics the commodified look of the woman in rapture*), in surrender to your "O baby let me masturbate you.I love to see your face when you cum"—your fingers like sand-paper rubbing at my soul.

Yes, but while I complied with your need my soul took in knowledge. Not just of you. But the bitterest knowledge: that how we are touched becomes the way we touch ourselves. And that this is how the soul dies—

(BLACKOUT)

SCENE FOUR—INNER STAGE

RISE: As lights rise the date 2002 is projected on curtain screen. As light rises on inner stage and date fades Jolie from outer stage rises and walks through curtain screen. Jonathan seated on bed, facing her. Jolie is now 12 years old.

JONATHAN
Did you wear it? The one I showed you?

JOLIE
(*Nods.*)

JONATHAN
Show me. Here, come into the light. Yes. Good. Now. Sit there. (*Indicates chair facing bed. She sits there, her back to the audience.*) Like that. Yes, with the robe like that, tied in the front. See how the light comes down across you now.
    (*He now sits on bed, facing her.*)

No. Don't move. Not yet. Now. Look at me now. Your face. I don't want to see anything but your face.

JOLIE
Dad please, not tonight. I hurt.

JONATHAN
You don't have to tell me it hurts. It has to. For a while. Soon. You'll see. Soon—this is what you're saying to yourself—pretty soon wet all the time, trust me, hungry all the time, like a big mouth, needing it, needing to feel the—

JOLIE
—Dad please, don't get angry. I . . . You don't under— . . . I can't . . . . It . . . You . . . Then it gets . . .

(BLACKOUT)

SCENE FIVE—OUTER STAGE

RISE: Adult Jolie as before, facing audience. As she begins Lights again go up in the house so that audience members become aware of one another.

JOLIE

—Dies into Lust—the pitched battle of equals out to deliver the wound that goes to the quick. Whattya think, ladies? They're big boys now, should we let them in on the secret? How there's always triumph from below. How a woman can make her body a corpse that kills. Or how a sharp twist and a howling in the hips can unman as surely as this deft reply to a casual but insistent question, "How good was it? I'd give it about a B-minus." Better yet the quick trip right after to the bathroom. To wash. Followed by the stupor sleep that ends all conversation save the one that plays on as he sits and smokes alone. Remember that strange satisfaction the first night he couldn't get it up? And all the ways you found to sustain the problem so you could watch confusion, frustration, then despair churn in him til he grabbed his cock, shook it like a sausage, and sweated it into a brief stand? Or the times you told him "I'm not in the mood tonight but you can if you want. It's like a mashed potato anyway, after the first push or two." Better yet the "please, please wait I'm almost there. No, not like that. I told you, if you wouldn't move like that when I'm almost there . . . . Try again? I can't. You know that. Not tonight."

(Lights in house go out.)

Take your pick. All roads lead to the crowning moment when he's high above you, pounding away, and you can hear it, the words, shouted or in the silence, the "here bitch I'll give it to you, the way you want it, you bitches all got some alley-cat in you." The ceremony of the dead, attained at last, bone to bone, socketed together, up and down, two hollowed out skulls, rubbing away at each other.

All that I was prepared to learn given my background. But nothing prepared me for what I learned when I tried, christ how I tried, believe me, tried, to make it work, to embrace the great institution marriage and say yes, if this is all one can hope for, to build a haven and nurture one another, slowly, carefully, only to find in it the worst. To feel touch die into normalcy and normalcy into contentment. It was then that I thought I was truly mad—suffocating in an unspeakable cruelty.

I know, I know, this isn't what you want, not the history you envisioned for me. You want me all dolled up in the latest symptoms—the affectless stare, the deadened body drooping like this, the head hanging lifeless, walking the dull round of its drift toward death. And on the inner screen too a sleepwalker moving like lead across a blank stage where nothing remains, no memory, except at times some after-image already fading then banished by the insistent flight from knowledge that defines your world. I tried. Believe me. But for me it never worked. Memory always stayed alive, avid—as image.

I remember, in high school, I'd lie awake—after—rigid but my mind racing, unable to halt the rush of images that projected themselves on the ceiling above me like pictures on a screen, a home movie superimposed on the idiot wallpaper Mitzi'd chosen for my room, a collage of Disneyfied monkeys, ducks, and mice grinning. It was like I was exploding out onto the ceiling, away from myself then back at myself in a whirl of images. But as dark shifted to shadow and become dawn I'd slow it down until there was a single picture, a snapshot preserved, refined, and stored here (*tapping head*) as a tablet against forgetting.

(BLACKOUT)

SCENE SIX—INNER STAGE

RISE: As lights rise on inner stage the date 2005 appears on the curtain screen. Jolie from outer stage rises and walks seductively through curtain screen and to Jonathan who is seated on bed waiting for her. She remains standing. Jolie is now 15 years old. As scene progresses lighting becomes expressionistic, nightmarish.

JONATHAN
Why are you dressed like that?

JOLIE
I thought you'd like it.

JONATHAN
That what you got with the money I gave you? I told you buy something nice. Your mother see you in that she'll—

JOLIE
—She helped me pick it out

JONATHAN
What for? A beauty pageant in the red-light district.

JOLIE
No. She's pretty much lost interest in all that now she's so fat. It's all Jesus now. Doesn't she tell you, about how He comes to her?

JONATHAN
I told you, we hardly talk anymore.

JOLIE
Pity. But look, how the cut of it angles—here.
 (She sits on chair, crosses legs.)

JONATHAN

Stop it. Think you look pretty with that muck all over your face?

JOLIE

Well it was quite a hit at school today, Jon.

JONATHAN

I told you, don't talk to me that way.
(*Pulls her up and moves her in front of the mirror.*)

C'mere, take a good look at yourself. With your face like that and your hair shooting out like some madwoman. Think I like it when you paint yourself up like this for me?

JOLIE

Who says it's for you, Jonathan? You're not the only one interested in how I look, you know. I have lots of admirers. If you only knew. All the boys—

JONATHAN

—Shut up. You know I hate it when you talk this way?

JOLIE

What way?

JONATHAN

Like you know so much.

JOLIE

Maybe I do. You know there's lots of things you don't know about. (*Pause.*) Awwh, what's wrong? Are you pouting? Why daddy, are you jealous? Silly man. I'm just teasing. You know my heart belongs to you. You're my daddy. I'll always be your little girl.

JONATHAN

I warned you not to start this shit with me again. Christ if you could see how pathetic you look. And you think men find this attractive.

JOLIE

(*Almost in reverie, the underlying panic emerging.*) It doesn't matter how I dress. They see it. At school, the boys. You should see the way they come around me in the halls. What I hear them saying. They see I'm different and they can't wait to find out how. It doesn't matter what I wear. That's Mitzi's idea. But you, you showed me different, Dad. I'm a big hit, thanks to you.

JONATHAN

(*Grabs her and pins her hands behind her back. From offstage a song begins to play, Mitzi's song, "Together," rising in volume during following.*)

Can't wait, can you? To feel their hands all over you. Fumbling around like jackals in your pussy? Your legs spread in the back seat of some car? The dress torn back. They don't even bother to take it off you know. The panties too. Is that the way you like it?
   (*The volume of the song now almost drowns him out. His voice rises in volume to it as he turns and addresses the offstage presence.*)

You with your idiot songs. Squatting there before your mirror. Mound of useless flesh. Laying there every night, like a beached whale. "Fuck me, Jonathan, please fuck me." Shit, I can't even stand the smell of you anymore—do you hear me?
   (*The volume of the song drowns him out. Long pause. He turns back to Jolie.*)

Maybe. Maybe on pimply little boys, but not on me. I'll learn you.

(BLACKOUT)

SCENE SEVEN—OUTER STAGE

RISE: *Adult Jolie as before, facing audience.*

JOLIE

I know the desire to forget, to shut down what beats here. (*Tapping forehead*) I tried, too—like you?—believe me I tried, to find my way to a deadened body and a life void of emotion. But I couldn't. Rage always supervened. And I knew that if I lost it, the rage, I'd lose myself. There'd be no me to open my hand in solidarity to all the others—like me—but broken by experiences I must believe were a thousand times worse than mine. Yes okay yes the fear that if I ever lose it . . . if this (*tapping forehead*) ever stops, then I truly will go mad. So okay yes I choose it: choose to remain without the thing I never had a chance to develop—a nice tight system of defenses. Choose it: to be no more than a medium; one whom experience enters utterly—my body its permanent record. For me memory can have nothing to do with forgetting—with bleaching things out and working them through. I am memory come alive—as act.

I'm sorry. You want events—don't you?—to round the story off to a fitting close. Me on the hook perhaps: "how better express her hatred of men." Or in porn: "look, look what she turned fucking into," pure gymnastics, the geometry of safety, the body like a piston, the face expressionless and wan, stiffening your prick's itch for the shower of cum to anoint me with your disgust. Okay. Okay. No more Sally Rand. The feathers drop away and I stand before you—the woman-child—in that pose you dote on. You know the one. Picasso invented it, Hefner perfected it. The buttocks full now and thrust out toward you, two orbs, plump and inviting. The shoulder turned so you can see the other at the same time—the left breast ripe, riding high, the nipple erect, waiting for the diddle of your thumb. The head spun round atop it, sitting there, holding itself there, in that dumb, insipid look you can't get enough of: the idiot grin that says "come, fuck me, any way you want me, I live just to please you." Okay. Picture this. The statue comes to life and turns on its axis so that at last she faces you. Courbet was a rank amateur. Finally. You get to see it. What you long for. A grown woman with the cunt of a little girl, shaven, open for your inspection so you can gape as long as you want—the image of your fascination, your horror, your obscure object of desire. Daddy was a true Cartesian—all he wanted was a little knowledge.

And you. What of you? Cause it's all theatre, isn't it? Health, Identity, the bonds of Love? I should know, I've been on stage since I was four. Oh, I know the great spirit of renewal that reigns here. The remarkable cures fashioned on this little O. The pity so readily extend. Your courage. Your desire to confront essential things. No violent emotion you won't applaud, no horror you won't bless, as long as it all leaves you purged when you leave, identity restored, world cleansed, all passion spent. I know. But I know something else: what a life under the bright lights taught me. That the art of acting begins on the other side of all that. And it's really simple—the art of acting. It can be condensed into an aphorism. *Something must break within with each line.* Because acting was shoved down my throat I had only one choice. To make it a portal of discovery. To take every role you offer me and find its hollowness. And then to play it—from here (*touches heart*)—so that you can know it too . . . if you want to . . . But for that to happen, something in you must break within with each line.

Everything you desire is visible to you here save the one thing you can't see. Except when something I do arrests you, for a moment, and you feel your world totter. That's when I get to look—for a change—and see dread in your eyes, as we meet in that place inside you that you never visit, that stage where all roles dissolve for they are nothing but dry straw (*snaps fingers*) consumed in an instant by what beats here. (*Taps head again.*)

In the dream it always happens after I've lived a long and honorable life. That's when they come to get me. The evidence has finally been unearthed, the body. I'm a murderer and yes of course the victim is always someone young, someone horribly violated. I buried the body in a field . . . deep . . . where no one could find it. But now they've dug it up and everyone knows.

The terrible thing about this dream: there's nothing surreal, dreamlike about it. This is not a vivid dream. The authorities who come to get me are ordinary in every way. The scene is blank. White. Fading. All I see now is myself in a room alone awaiting an interrogation that has already taken place, begging the same empty room with a plea that I know has already been rejected, unheard.

What's terrible about this dream is its lack of color. It has the absolute certainty of fact. And that knowledge is so unassailable that whenever the dream happens I spend the next day trying to convince myself the dream isn't true. The day becomes a dream—everything real recedes and I walk through it as one trying vainly to come back, to reattach myself to the world. I always succeed—eventually. The dream fades. I forget again and live—until. Then I'm in a room alone again knowing that nothing else is.

That's it, isn't it? This dream. It's the stage, the backdrop to all my other dreams, the motive for their intense imaginings. But this dream needs no fireworks. It's more powerful than any other dream because it's true. And I can never convince myself it isn't, because I know it is.

The feeling tone of it, you ask? Unremitting. Yes of course I know what the dream means. No inquiry is needed there.
(*Here she breaks down in a sobbing that lasts through the following lines.*)

That I did it—to myself. The pageants. To myself, ten cents a dance. That I would do anything—to win your love. That you let me do it. Saw I was doing it and couldn't stop yourselves. I was a child, how could you let me do that to myself—
(*Now directly, to the audience.*)

Yeh yeh yeh yeh yeh yeh yeh. I know. I know. A child can't understand things this way. Can't be held responsible. That would

be too cruel, wouldn't it? Besides, it's only a dream. Who would dare suggest that we are responsible for our dreams? Because if that's true, children are the only ones who know how precious life is—know it at the very moment they sacrifice it.
   (*She now turns and faces a man who has come on stage during the foregoing and who stands there waiting, observing.*)

All right, Josh. You. You knew I'd get around to you.

(*Goes directly into next scene without Blackout.*)

SCENE EIGHT—OUTER STAGE

(*This scene must be staged and played in such a way that the audience senses that they are still inside her head, that the play is memory and thus is able here to condense in one scene of imagined conversation the pain, bitterness, and regret that eats away at the heart when a genuine love is lost. It is almost as if the two characters are speaking alone together, addressing the other, after long painful reflection, saying finally what one was never able to say before and must say in order to be free.*)

JOSH
On cue, baby. The post-mortem. Scene you do best. Last chance to firm up whatever lie you need to tell yourself to keep your great quest going.

JOLIE
Is that all you can do? After what we had. Come here to play another of your word games.

JOSH
You drained me of everything else.

JOLIE
Drained you. I opened to you. That's what you couldn't stand.

JOSH
What I couldn't stand was your need to keep re-opening your precious wound.

JOLIE
Just once. Can't we? Without the bullshit? Touch what we had and speak from there. Maybe then we can make a clean break and be free of it. Remember, when we vowed we'd live it out it—together—touch, all it revealed. You told me it was the one thing you believed in.

JOSH
So did you. Wherever it led.

JOLIE
I never betrayed that.

JOSH
Yes you did.

JOLIE
No. You. When you started to touch me like that. Like you were probing—trying to find new ways I needed to be healed—

JOSH
—Find them. Christ, you couldn't wait to announce them—

JOLIE
—It just took me a long time to catch on, Josh. Even then—five years ago—remember, when touch was discovery, even then your fingers were filing away another record, weren't they? Priming me for something else? You were always a double agent, Josh.

JOSH
Not in the beginning. It wasn't like that, Jo, believe—

JOLIE
—Don't call me that.

JOSH
Whatever. All I felt, in the beginning, was my heart opening—in tenderness—toward you. That was the only thing in my hand when I touched you. Even after I saw you'd need to turn it into another piece of knowledge, another "inquiry."

JOLIE
Knowledge. I thought that was your thing. But you weren't after knowledge, were you? Not my kind, the kind that opens you up and leaves you open. WHY? What was it you couldn't bear, Josh? When everywhere, in my body, I remember how you were at first, when you touched me and my heart came. How could you let that die?

JOSH
Die. Shit, all I did was try to protect us from your need to twist every experience until you find the same cruelty everywhere. Think I couldn't feel it, when you'd pull apart into that voracious mind of yours and lie there, watching me, your body poised for the one moment I'd touch you in a way that turned me into the others? Him? My betrayal. You don't believe in anything but betrayal. Like when we went through your "I've just got to get it out" phase. When all I could say—to one attack after another—"you're talking to someone else. Not me. Saying to me what you failed to say to them. To him." Why couldn't you be with me, goddammit, and not with someone else?

JOLIE
What was I supposed to do, Josh? What is love if it doesn't uproot everything dead inside? When it all broke inside me . . . I knew that had to happen. That there was something here (*indicating body*) I needed to know so I could bring it back and open it—to

you. When I couldn't come back . . . I was alone then in a way I'd never been before.

JOSH
Sure, like that time, three days running, when you kept playing that fucking Alanis Morisette CD over and over, drinking yourself into a vodka stupor. I can still hear the jumps, the damn thing playing on, stuck in the same track, over and over. Or the times you lay there, in that bed, like a corpse—except for the eyes, darting about then staring at something, nothing in the corner of the room—

JOLIE
—At—

JOSH
—At bullshit. At a lot of cheap theatrics. But I stayed, didn't I? I held you when I could and I waited with you when I couldn't.

JOLIE
You stayed all right. Another chance for your beneficent cock to find the moment when you could make everything right.

JOSH
As if you could change any of it. You can't. It's not in your "nature!"

JOLIE
Nature. You coward. You, who were so free once. What turned you against yourself? You think I couldn't feel it, when your touch changed?

JOSH
Here we go again. Another one of your privileged insight into the world of touch.

JOLIE
No. Because it wasn't there—at first. Know how I knew something

had changed? When you kept making your little inquiries. About the others. And about what he did. There was a panic in you, Josh. You want to talk about nature. Let's talk about your nature.

JOSH
My "nature" was that I loved you and couldn't stand the competition you set up between me and your precious wound. You don't know what it was like. To lay there and feel you flowing away to some other place where I could never be with you. I just wanted to hold you, for a while.

JOLIE
You shouldn't lie to yourself like that, Josh. You were after something else and you know it. Power. The power of sex to bind me to you. Tenderness, that was your weapon. But worship—that's what you were after. From the beginning! Why? That's the only question worth asking, Josh. Why?

JOSH
I gather you're about to tell me. To call on your superior knowledge and—

JOLIE
It's not important that I know—

JOSH
—what I know is I loved you. There was no other agenda.

JOLIE
Yes, you loved me, but you wanted it all to close on itself like a ball of energy you could hold in your hand. Christ, Josh, it was you who helped me discover it, that touch only stays alive when it accepts everything that rises up inside whenever we love someone. I thought I knew what was in here waiting to get me. What I knew was nothing to what I learned loving you.

JOSH
Yeh—and what was that?

JOLIE
That there's nothing more terrifying than to be touched in tenderness by someone you love. I was safe with the others. They never touched me. They fucked whatever image of me—no, of themselves fucking me—they had to get in their heads so that they could cum. But you, Josh, you got to the heart of me. But then you had to "appropriate" it, didn't you?. That's what I can't forgive. We took it, sex, and bent it to everything courageous in us. And then you pissed on that. To protect yourself. To turn it into another adventure with the dark side of your cock. So you can stay safe in that elegant prison you've fashioned for yourself. But not alone! You wanted to be sure that when the door shut I'd be in there with you. On my knees. Another sleeping beauty ready to cum on cue to the sexual Messiah.

JOSH
You were always quite a phrase-maker "Jo." (*She ignores name this time.*) But we're into your specialty now. Fuck, I was just another piece of ass to you. Another step in your "inquiry." You drained me dry. Of everything, goddammit.

JOLIE
Oh, that's why you needed the others. Cause you were dry.

JOSH
Yes.

JOLIE
Or because you were hungry for another famous victory.

JOSH
I told you. The others were nothing to me—after you. But it served it's purpose, didn't it? Gave you a reason to split.

JOLIE
As if they mattered. The self-betrayal. That's what hurt, here (*touching heart*) long before you staged the oldest, tritest comedy to make your exit.

JOSH
You're the one who left me. Remember, when you couldn't get enough of it. Those nights we fucked—again and again—and lay there, apart and sullen in the times between. Then desperate for it. For what you're always after—a new encounter with the disorder at the heart of your sex.

JOLIE
My new encounter. I'll give it to you. You've earned it. What opened up in me, when we touched. I don't know if it's there anymore. That's what happens now, when I try to feel us again, if only for the one flaming instant. But now I always cry then, weeping when I cum. A new kind of fucking, that's what you've given me. And it works so well I don't even know about the past anymore. Maybe I was dead long before you. But you, pal, you knew how to screw the lid down. Why? Why couldn't you stay with me there, in that place where we touch a solitude we can't do anything about—but accept it. You don't know, do you? All your insight into yourself and on that one you draw a blank. How convenient.

(*He moves as if to interrupt.*)

No. Please. Let me say this. Once. Remember, when you told me about it. On one of those long nights when we were first together, when we lay there together talking all night. When love is the need to say all the forgotten things that come back in a rush because you love someone. Remember, when you were two, living with your mother at her parents' house and she took you on a trip to visit your father at that Navy Base in Wildwood.

JOSH
I knew you'd bring that up. Yeh, I remember. The night she left

me alone for the first time, sleeping in a crib while they went to the room next door. I told you—didn't I? Fucking idiot! How whenever I'd cry her mother—"grandma"—would rush into the room, yelling at her, and shove a bottle in my mouth because one of her inane Irish beliefs was "babies should not be allowed to cry." You loved that one, didn't you? How I woke that night in the dark, crying for her to come and hold me as she always did . . . .

JOLIE
And she didn't come.

JOSH
Yeh yeh how the cry became louder for her in the dark. Yeh, I remember. How I couldn't breathe and I couldn't stop it, the crying, louder and louder out of me. The crib it was like hot plastic. I was suffocating in it, thrashing about until I found the bars of it and dragged myself up, over the top of it, onto something hard and cold.

JOLIE
(*She here reaches out and touches him for the only time in the scene.*)

Don't stop, Josh, please.

JOSH
(*He pulls away*) My face was burning up—all sweat and tears—and still I couldn't stop it, the crying, even when I made my hands fists and pounded in the dark down on the hard cold thing. There was nothing but the black—closing in on me—nothing. Just a cry in a black nothing when they finally came and found me there like that, on the top of a dresser, shaking my fists, screaming . . . Yeah, I remember. So what? So fucking what?

JOLIE
Cause it was then, Josh, that your psyche was born, one with its founding terror. No, I don't mean any of that primal scream bullshit,

and you know it. Everything you opened to me in the great rush of our love to be the one flame embracing forever. All we wanted to be. All we lost. It all began that night when you first felt death enter you. (*Pause.*) Do you know what you have to do? You have to find your way back into that room. And without the lie that you use touch for anything but to compel the teat—no, excuse me, the cunt—to render its juice as a promise never to leave you alone again.

JOSH

What poetry!

JOLIE

—fuck you.

JOSH

Yeh and fuck you too. Have any idea what it was like to feel it—here (*jabbing at heart with index finger*)—the one message you make clear from the start. Don't tie me down. I'm a wolf blah blah blah . . . My fear! Fuck, do you have any idea what it was like to compete with that.

(*In what follows their lines overlap as each drifts into monologue and speaks their need only half hearing what the other says.*)

JOLIE

There was no competition. Only the love—

JOSH

—to know that all you felt, knew when we made love: that I could never come close to experiencing that—

JOLIE

—you betrayed the minute you stopped opening yourself to me . . .

JOSH

—and so no way to stop you from taking what we found there—

together—and withdrawing into that place where you're always alone, preparing yourself for some action that holds me, everyone, in contempt.

JOLIE

—Cause that's the only way. Love—the chance to get at the dead place in us and rip it open, to possibility, to what we are, can be, whenever we make love. That's what we did.

JOSH

—As if I anything but a dildo to comfort you whenever you got scared of yourself.

JOLIE

—Together, before you killed it for that coward who's always hiding in your touch, that little prick who needs to turn every room into a stage where an angry child, seeking applause, compels Mama to stay rapt, in adoration, wet for you.
(This last line brings him back and all that follows is now said directly, face to face.)

JOSH

How convenient. I'm always on stage like you, huh? Like you, singing "my heart belongs to daddy." Fucking—then "after" making it up to Daddy for cheating on him.

JOLIE

Touche.

JOSH

Yeh, and what room are you afraid of, Jo?
(This time she doesn't object to the name.)

JOLIE

Don't worry. If I ever get there you'll only be one of the props.

JOSH

Yeh, well I gave you a good fucking, didn't I? Face it, that's all you were really after.

JOLIE

That's the thing about you, Josh, you always know how to give what you need.

JOSH

And you . . . what do you need?

JOLIE

Need? I need you like I need another fuck.
(*She turns from him. Looks toward audience. Pauses, as if to repeat last line to them. Returns to chair she was sitting on at the beginning of the play. Sits. Lights cigarette. Pauses. Then reaches out. Takes up book. Opens it. Begins Reading. Very low, almost inaudible beginning of music that will play in.*)

(BLACKOUT)

(*In Blackout the music slowly changes as her memory now bleeds into what happened five years previously. The music becomes the music from the orchestral section in the last movement of Mahler's* **Das Leid von der Erde**, *the section called Der Abschied (The Farewell) This music plays on intermittently in the following scene.*)

SCENE NINE—INNER STAGE

RISE: The words **Five Years Before** *are visible on the curtain screen which remains drawn across the inner stage. There, center stage, a couple sits, unclothed, but with blankets around them, facing each other, their legs intertwined, the woman asleep, her head resting on the man's shoulder. In the action that follows two people seek—through touch—to address the wound in the other, to make the act of love the* *effort to open, confront, and overcome the conflicts that define our psychosexual identity, conflicts that are lived—in the body—whenever we actually touch or are touched by another with love. Language is thus secondary to what happens here and the actors must strive to make it so, finding in gesture, motion, touch the actions necessary to complete the dialogue. But all this must be done with the greatest delicacy and tenderness. Sex is here the ecstatic celebration of the bond created by two agents as they hold and touch each other, weep in one another's arms, cry out their anger, their anguish, and their astonished amazement at the power of sexual love to awaken that which is most traumatic in us and create from it the body of eros.*

JOLIE
(*A whimper and then a stifled crying out. She awakes. Pulls back.*)

JOSH
You were asleep.

JOLIE
(*Surprised.*) I was.

JOSH
—Are you cold?

JOLIE
No . . . A little maybe. You?

JOSH
Yes. I sweat so . . . and now . . .

JOLIE
Let me hold you. Warm you.

JOSH
(*Drawing back*) Want something to eat, some fruit, cheese?

JOLIE
No. Don't go. Stay. Like this. I love to be with you like this, baby.

JOSH
You were trembling.

JOLIE
I know. Sometimes—it just happens. And then I can't do anything about it. You didn't have to stop, baby, it would've been allright.

JOSH
I can't, like that. It doesn't matter. To hold you like this, Jo. It's more than enough.

JOLIE
I love it, Josh, the way you touch me. It's like . . . I feel like I'm almost shy with you . . . But it's terrible, too, to feel myself opening to you like this. (*Reaches for cigarette*) It's like there's something inside me, cutting at me, at all the places where you touch me. (*She starts to pull back.*) It's broken loose. He's broken lose.
 (*He touches her, cautiously.*)

JOSH
Can I hold you now? Just hold you—

JOLIE
—No. Not now. (*He starts to move away.*) No, Baby, don't go. Just be with me here—like this (*Pause, during which she lights cigarette.*) Christ, I hate it when I get like this, I want you to know that. Hate the—

JOSH
Sshhh . . . (*During following lines touches her face gently. She glows.*) It's all right. I love it, to hold you. To touch your face—so smooth . . . your skin like silk, your—
 (*Touching her breast. She pulls away.*)

JOLIE
—Don't. The place I go. Inside. When it breaks. You can't be with me there. Ever.

JOSH
I know.

JOLIE
But you want to. I can feel it. You have to let me go then.

JOSH
I can't. That's where I love you, where I want to love you.

JOLIE
Don't.
(*She sits silent, with cigarette, withdrawn. He reaches back for wine bottle. Fills her glass, his own.*)

JOSH
You know what those cigarettes do to me.

JOLIE
I'm sorry. But I need them, to be sharp now. (*Tapping head.*) That's why I try to stay awake—after. When I sleep it's like a razor cutting at me—there. Slicing off parts of me.
(*He reaches out to caress her face. She shakes her head. Pause. Then a new movement outward to him, and with it a renewed struggle with the traumatic conflicts that are inseparable from her sexual being.*)

Christ, I want to, believe me. The way you touch me. Never, before, like this. So gentle, your lips. The way you hold my breast, so tender. And then when you take me in your mouth—there—I feel myself opening all over, in tenderness toward you. You're different. You know that don't you. Not like most men. Touch me again now baby. (*She here takes his hand and puts it between her legs.*) Yes, gently, like that.

JOSH

I love you, Jo. (*Now slowly moving down*) Christ, woman, sometimes I just want to lay with you like this and sleep, the whole night, like this, to smell you like the rich damp earth in springtime—

JOLIE

—yes baby, it's like your tongue is kissing me there, in my soul.
  (*She here pulls him up and kisses him in a long embrace. Then speaking with some urgency, fighting off rising panic within.*)

But now every time Josh when you're in me . . . the other thing, it's like a knot, a knot that wants to close like a vice and squeeze the life out of you. (*Starts to weep, quietly.*) Does it hurt you then baby? O Christ I'm so sorry if I hurt you then.

JOSH

No. No. Don't worry. Anything that happens, everything, is all right. We're one here Jo, one—

JOLIE

—I want you in me now, Josh. To feel you in me—the way you are when you're in me. Touching me there in all the places where I need you. Need you there like a tongue licking at fire in me. (*Suddenly pulls back*) Aahh the, goddammit, Josh, goddamn them, the fucking . . . all the time now it's like when I sleep. It can't wait now. He can't. She.
  (*From here on she has trouble breathing; choking sensation at times, as she re-lives in her body what she tries to put into words.*)

It's like a pane of glass cutting right across my voice. It sticks there, the glass. And then I feel it slicing, the pane of glass, moving slow right through my throat.
  (*Here uncontrollably starts shaking her head back and forth as the following lines break from within her.*)

"No, you fuck you fucking fuck I'll . . . You . . . I—

(*He reaches forward to comfort her. Her head hits his: it's like a slap across her own face, waking her from trance state.*)

Oh baby . . . Did I hurt you, baby? (*weeping*) I'm so sorry—

JOSH
No, no. It's allright.
(*She now embraces him passionately with her whole body, straining to go on.*)

No. No more. We can't now, we—(*in some alarm, stops, pulls away*) I can't. I'm afraid—afraid I'll hurt you. We have to stop.

JOLIE
No. This is where we can't stop. I want to open it all to you, Josh. To tear away at what is dead in me. To rip him out of me. Her. Everything they did. When you touch me I melt inside, but then they erupt everywhere, at me, stabbing, choking. (*Pause*) If I can tighten and close then you can tear at me but never touch me. No. I won't. (*to her parents and in voice of child*) "I don't care what YOU do." I want you, Josh, my body one with you . . . turning myself inside out to you . . . there . . . in the place where you can kill me.

JOSH
No, where there's nothing but you and me touching each other, like a line of energy coursing through me into you—into the heart of you—

JOLIE
Yes baby, like you're opening too inside me. Like a tongue kissing me in all the places where I want you. Where I need you. Yes, like that, baby, love me like that—

JOSH
—all of myself—into you. Into my love for you.
(*He touches her gently on the face. Then draws his head up to her.*)

They kiss, embrace—long, slow. As the kiss blossoms, their bodies striving to be one, he reaches climax.)

JOLIE
(*To Jonathan and Mitzi—in traumatic regression but also in defiance*) "No. Not yet, can't you bastards goddamn you let me . . ." Yes baby like that. Hold me like that. Love me like that. Yes baby please yes.

(*She reaches climax in the full ecstasy of her courageous refusal to be defeated. Simultaneous with it the beginnings of an assault from within as traumatic memories course through her body. She trembles. He stirs, as if to pull away.*)

No. Stay. Like this. Talk to me now, while I can still feel you throbbing in me.

JOSH
Yes, while I can feel you opening and closing around me. To touch you now, your beautiful open face that hides nothing . . . You're the greatest adventure, baby.

JOLIE
My life, everything I've done, has been to get here, to be with you here like this. But it's terror this—to open my body to you like this.

JOSH
I'll never hurt you, you know that don't you?

JOLIE
It doesn't matter. There's no way to protect myself anymore. He was wrong—Rilke. There's no solitude anymore. No place left where we can't do permanent damage to each other. You're in me now. In my deepest solitude there's only you—

JOSH

—where I love you

JOLIE

—No place I'll go that won't bring me back here to you.

JOSH

—where I'll never hurt you.

JOLIE

—where you'll always hurt me. I ask only one thing. If you know you have to . . . to hurt me here (*indicating sexual body*)—in that way. Leave me. I won't resent it. I'll understand. I'll even be proud. That we knew the limit and refused to do the other thing.

JOSH

Jo, if you only knew. When I touch you now, sometimes all I touch is my fear of losing you. (*Pause, lighting cigarette.*) You're different too you know. I knew it—the first time . . . what you said. I could see it, in your face—some inner process had completed itself. You looked at me, with a frankness I'd never seen before. Do you remember what you said? "I'm ready to make love with you." With. A simple preposition. But one I'd never heard a woman say before—in that context.

(*His need to withdraw kicks in.*)

You know where most of them betray themselves? When they first feel touched—in a way they've never been touched before—they decide that because you touched them like that it means they're the one woman you've been searching for your whole fucking life. And once that happens, it's curtains. Cause then they can never let go. A single sentence, keeps repeating itself, over and over, in their heads: "He loves me, only he doesn't know it yet." Nothing you say can dislodge that one. And so the charade—the months of shame disguised as anger then that long-suffering look they get when they forgive you, again and again, cause all they want is to give you the time you need so you can discover that you "really love them." The fucking bovine stupidity, that's what—

JOLIE

Please, Josh. Don't. You don't have to talk like this to impress me. I know you. From the way you touch me. You're a kind and gentle man. We can be that—together. The other crap, we don't need it anymore.

(*Pause, then defying her own inner panic.*)

Do you know how wolves make love? The female chooses and it only happens when she's ready. The male enters her then, but without urgency. No baring of the fangs. No wrenching back of her head. No frenzied thrusting. Once he's in her they lay there like that ... quietly ... for the better part of an hour, during which, I'm told, he has repeated orgasms *with* a female who stays keen, open to him. The only sad part is their faces. They stay turned away. They can't see each other. Maybe that's in keeping with some commandment: to stop them from staying there like that forever. Let's break it. Come inside me again—face to face—and see what glows here when you're in me.

(*She sits astride him. There is at first a panic in him, a fear he won't be able. But no urgency. No manipulation by either. Instead, he just looks in her face. And then love rises in him. Entwined like that, she bends to kiss him as the act ends with this purely physical tableau to music from the end of the final section of Mahler's* Song of the Earth; *to the words "Ewig."(Forever). Lights slowly dim on them to*

(BLACKOUT)

ACT THREE—THE DOOR TO SUMMER

SCENE ONE—THE SCOTTISH PLAY

RISE: The year 2030 visible on curtain screen. Act to be played on Outer Stage. Three a.m. Lighting to reflect this. Mitzi, in chair, Stage Right, looking into mirror—facing the audience, putting on then taking off make-up, false eyelashes, wigs, even disposable eyes that she inserts after squeezing hypo-tears into her eyes: a woman of seventy trying to look fifty. Then in the dark from Stage Left we hear a sharp cry of pain followed by a wailing. Mitzi pauses, dismisses the sound, returns to her work. Slowly lights come up on Jonathan, in pyjamas, pacing, weeping. Eventually, but without apparently hearing him, Mitzi turns as if on cue, rises, walks to center stage, stands staring at him.

MITZI

Again?

JONATHAN

Yes.

MITZI

What can I do for you?

JONATHAN
Nothing.

MITZI
Are you sure?

JONATHAN
Yes. Let's get to work. It's always better after. There's a shitload of legal papers. And the finances for the Jolie Brady Children's Foundation—a mess. We drew off too much for legal fees. The only thing keeping it afloat is contributions from the Christian groups.

MITZI
Not now, Jonathan. Please. Our Christmas TV visit—when we invite all of America into our home. Can't we work on that first? It just didn't have that warm feeling last year. Like when we first moved here. So *tres jolie*. That's what I'm best at Jonathan—at creating something cultured and refined, to celebrate the season.

JONATHAN
The media people have nixed the Christmas visit, Mitzi. It just brings up the old questions. And frankly, m'dear, it's become dull even to you.

MITZI
Not at the end Jonathan. Not when I get to say Mrs. Nixon's line: "I treat each day as Christmas." I feel it then, the whole audience reaching out to embrace us.

JONATHAN
The audience. Right. There's where we've got work to do. The annual Barbara Walters interview . . . To celebrate Barbara's 100th birthday. We need a Brush up bad. It's all drying up. Your timing's way off. You're starting to gush again.

MITZI
And why is that Jonathan? Because I'm all alone out there. You don't give me anything I can work off of. You're back in your Perry Como pose—all aloof and controlled.

JONATHAN
That's because you're the old Mitzi again, emoting on every line. (*Mimics her manner in what follows.*) "There's a killer out there. Look to your babies. Gather them close to you." Christ. That crap doesn't play worth a damn anymore.

MITZI
Well somebody's got to get some emotion into it. You're so laid back you're fading into the wallpaper. (*She now switches and tries to play the director, to prompt him.*) Remember when you used to get angry and lash out at them.

JONATHAN
Yeh, that stuff was fine, in the beginning, when we were hounded by the tabloids, with those videos of her everywhere. (*Indicating audience*) Now it just pisses them off. Rule number one: you don't get an audience to take your side by offending them. You've got to change with their needs. Find what's called the *arc of their needs*, and shape an interview so that everything builds to how you want them to feel at the end. You don't spill emotions. You milk them.

MITZI
Give me something to play off and I'll milk it, bub. I know how to work an audience. I learned all about that long before you pal—

JONATHAN
—you learned how to keep red-necks hot and bothered. That's the problem. You've got one emotional key—you gush. And then you can't stop. What did the media people try to teach you—from day

one? You're a grieving mother for chrissake not some prima donna doing *Lucia*. Remember the videos they showed you of Jackie. Dignified grief. "Feel the emotion, don't show it." THAT'S ACTING! Remember how you used to do the lie detector bit? How you paused with your hand on your breast, like you couldn't breathe momentarily, choking back tears. But you didn't give in to it. Remember, you paused and then you told them how just before you went in to take the test you closed your eyes and saw her face. You paused again—with that flutter you get. Then you said the line, your voice cracking. "I'm doing this for you, baby." Now that was a fucking masterpiece! I took a peek at the audience. You had 'em. You never came closer to turning it all around.

(*Often, on appropriate lines, from here on both gesture out to the audience, inviting them to take their side.*)

MITZI

But none of it works if I'm playing the scene with a stiff, Jonathan. You're so into your "new career" as a Director, you've forgotten it worked because we were a perfect team. Every time I choked up, you stepped in—and with some fire in your belly. An audience needs more than all this cerebral crap. You say I gush, but I feel it . . . the men out there—"wow, she's on fire . . . that's real passion." They want me! That makes your job easier. But you gotta give the ladies something too. You're the man—you need to be forceful, indignant. Your family's been made mock of by the media. Your child ravaged by some monster. "There's a killer out there"— and still THEY keep persecuting US. But not you, Jonathan. Well here's a new flash, bud, the Mr. Cool routine's not doing your image any favors. And now, criminnie, to top it you've got me giving statistics about the scientific validity of lie detector tests. There's no feeling in that!

JONATHAN

THERE IS IF YOU PLAY IT RIGHT. What you can't get through your head is statistics is what they want now. What they've wanted for a long time. To wash their hands of all the tabloid stuff.

MITZI
—No. I won't let them. After what they said. Those terrible stories about child abuse. Why sometimes, Jonathan, I don't care, I just want to lash out at all of them!

JONATHAN
But then you lose the *arc*! Our job now is to take away their guilt. The scientific shit does that. If you knew the first thing about audiences you'd understand it all changed that day—remember the tape I showed you—when Dan Rather ended his special with the line: (*Mimicking Rather*) "And there are those videos, which some people *unfortunately* find provocative."

MITZI
The vultures. They stole them. Those videos were private, for the families only. Pageant participants know that—

JONATHAN
—Stop gushing. You miss the point. Listen to the last five words. Rather's telling "the American people!" how to feel. How to prove their virtue. NO MORE PRURIENT INTERESTS! (*Snaps fingers*) And like magic, since that day there's been nary a word about the sex stuff. It's all a whodunit now. All footprints and cobwebs and stun—guns. And the beauty of that scenario, dear heart, is that nothing can ever be proved. Dueling experts—and Pouf—it all blows away. Shit, frankly, I find most of the scientific stuff boring—

MITZI
—It's not fair! They shouldn't be allowed to forget. What they did. To our perfect family. That's what Geraldo called us. Turned us into a laughing stock.

JONATHAN
Fine. Fine. But restrain it. Make it work. Blame the media. Blame Freud. Blame the loss of family values, if you must. But do it in a way that offers them absolution! Look, audiences are like children.

Each emotion they have is like a little spasm. They're not like you. They don't see emotions as arias. They've got one need—to get rid of anything that causes them pain. Sure, they want the peep show. That's why they're here. They're afraid to live, but they can't get enough of it second hand. But then when it comes, it's too much for them. That's where the *arc* comes in. See, the trick is to put them in an emotional bind so that when relief is offered they rush to embrace it!

MITZI

You've become quite the director haven't you?

JONATHAN

I didn't read all that theatre crap for nothing. (*Then, almost as an aside*) But it's funny. It gave me what I always wanted. A way to understand what people feel—why they feel.

MITZI

Mother always said you might "grow a brain someday. But that's all you are, buster. Take a look at your recent public appearances. You're fading into the back wall.

JONATHAN

That's the point. They want it all to fade away now, like a bad dream. That's why the videos are all safely locked away in a vault at the Foundation. All that's left is Jolie as she was—a beautiful, innocent child.

MITZI

Yes. She had that glow. Like a thousand angels weaved themselves in her hair and Jesus himself smiled in her eyes. The loss of her . . . it WAS *The Loss of Innocence*.

JONATHAN

There! (*Snapping fingers, from this point on the confident director.*) That's the key. Keep your eye on that idea—the whole interview—

and the right emotions will flow. That way when we get to the center of it—to the lines we've worked on so long—it'll all click.

MITZI
But only if you give ME the hot coals line, Jonathan.

JONATHAN
Okay, okay, but don't make it a travesty. Play it slow, deliberate, almost like you're offering them (*points out toward audience*) a challenge but one that good, sympathetic people must refuse. Here, try it. I'll cue you. (*Cueing her*) "Passing the lie detector tests should have been enough . . ." Now hold the pause . . . Then.

MITZI
"What do you want us to do, walk on hot coals?"

JONATHAN
No. Don't wince the line. It's not about how hot coals would feel on your precious feet. It's about them—their cruelty. About all we've gone through to prove our innocence. The key is to make the righteous indignation play on their sympathies. That's what hit me, the day that line came to me: the perfect tone of it. (*Snaps fingers.*) Try it again.

MITZI
(***Repeats the line***) *Passing the lie detector tests should have been enough. What do you want us to do, walk on hot coals?*

JONATHAN
Better. Look, it's like your (*here mimics her, with finger pointed at audience*) "don't go there" line. But played not as a threat but as an invitation. That's how you create sympathy. Let them know we've had enough persecution, but don't offend them—

MITZI
Like this: (***She now repeats the line perfectly.***) *Passing the lie detector*

tests should have been enough. What do you want us to do, walk on hot coals? But it only works, Jonathan, if you don't rush in right away. Look, after I finish, hold your line for a full beat . . . No two . . . So the camera has time to linger on me—on my face, my pain. Then, slowly, hold it up—the snapshot of her.
(She takes the snapshot up from table and mimics for Jonathan the action he is to perform. She then hands snapshot to him and he performs the correct movement with it.)

That's right. Like that. Then wait. Wait for the camera to move in on the photo then back out until your face is framed with hers. *(Snaps fingers to cue.)*

JONATHAN

(Looking directly at audience) "This is the child who was taken from us. Brutally. There's a killer out there—and we won't rest until we've found you."

MITZI

Yes, yes! If you can make your voice crack like that. But with authority, too. And anger—you've got to get some anger into it. You're dignified—but also tireless in the pursuit of Justice!

JONATHAN

(Repeats the lines perfectly.) This is the child who was taken from us. Brutally. There's a killer out there—and we won't rest until we've found you.

MITZI

(Taking that cue she now matches to his lines her pre-planned facial expressions.)

Yes, that's it. Cause then they'll see it as the camera moves back to me. How your words have taken me all the way back.—to our dear lost child. The camera can't leave me now. It's all over me. My lips tremble. My eyes tear up. You put your arm around me, ever so gently, on my shoulder. To comfort me. No, slow. Yes, like that.

JONATHAN
We hold that pose. Then ever so slowly you incline your head down as if to cradle it on my shoulder. But then you stop. The last note must be your inner strength despite the pain. Our endurance—together—that's the image we leave them with.

MITZI
Good. Let's try it. From the Top.

(*They now repeat the dialogue and gestures of the rehearsed scene from start to finish.*)

MITZI
Passing the lie detector tests should have been enough. What do you want us to do, walk on hot coals?

JONATHAN
This is the child who was taken from us. Brutally. There's a killer out there—and we won't rest until we've found you.

(*At end Mitzi is so moved that she drops her head to his shoulder and turns it up with that dreamy look, awaiting an embrace.*)

JONATHAN
I told you, can the gushy shit. It's never enough for you, is it? Have to milk everything to feed your emotional needs.

MITZI
And you to withdraw every time I feel close to you. Like now when you said the lines about her. I felt like we could finally put it all behind us and go on.

JONATHAN
—To what? Another addition to the house? Another week with you on a beach in Aruba? Everything I do just makes you hungrier. Like your sainted mother loved to say: (*mimics Pauline*) "Jonathan's job is to earn the money, ours is to spend it."
(*They now start cutting angrily into each other's lines, repeating a tired yet lethal litany.*)

MITZI
—as if it didn't give you what you want. A chance to bitch to your friends and retreat to your corner—

JONATHAN
—Anything for a little peace from the Princess Mitzi routine. The incessant nagging. Until I get you what you want—THIS WEEK!

MITZI
—So you can sit there with that superior air, smirking at my family, at everything I've done to bring culture into this home.

JONATHAN
Culture. You call this crap culture. The taste of a vulgarian. It's all over the top. Empty and desperate—like your emotions. Like the way you fuck!

MITZI
—You pig, when I was the trophy you needed to complete your image. What all you wimps want the minute you get rich. "'I'm an ugly, gutless man. But I just bought me a beautiful, classy woman. Therefore I'm not ugly. Everyone wants to fuck my wife." Don't kid yourself, you loved it, rubbing my pussy in the nose of greater Boulder.

JONATHAN
What, like that absurd surprise party you concocted for your fortieth birthday. And Christ I had to keep up the pretense it was my idea. What an enchanted evening. Everybody dancing to the

bottomless pit of your needs. Everybody. Even her. My little girl. Even she wasn't safe. You had to turn her into some copy of yourself, dressing her up in costumes like you wore when you were Miss West By God Virginia. And then, you fucking bitch, that feather number you paraded her around in like you couldn't wait to pimp your own daughter to every sick fuck in the country—

                        MITZI
You loved it. The proud father. His flesh—what they all want a piece of. Daddy's little girl . . . all pink and white. I dressed her allright. You're the one who—

                        JONATHAN
—Don't go there.

                        MITZI
Eye of the beholder, Jon.
    (*Both now freeze, knowing that something has once again run its nightly course.*)

                        MITZI
Enough?

                        JONATHAN
Yes, enough.
    (*Both now get a strangely satisfied look. What had to happen has. The Ritual can therefore commence.*)

                        MITZI
Good.

                        JONATHAN
Yes.

                        MITZI
It's time?

                    JONATHAN
Yes.

                    MITZI
Good. Is it ready?

                    JONATHAN
Yes. I rewound it before we went to bed.

> (*They now sit together on a couch, Center Stage. He flicks a switch and on the curtain screen we see, with the Bradys, an actual video of JonBenét Ramsey, aged six, performing "Cowboy's Sweetheart." The stage darkens, making the audience's position identical to Jonathan and Mitzi's. After a time, abruptly, the film whirls then stops, snaps, a slash moves through it, the image burns up. The stage is then flooded with the brightest, whitest light imaginable. Jolie, aged 45, stands in pool of light. They turn to her.*)

SCENE TWO—THE STONE GUEST

                    MITZI
Baby, is it you? O JuJuBee, I've missed you so.

                    JONATHAN
My little girl . . . She's come back—

                    MITZI
—Oh baby, I knew He'd hear me someday, Jesus, when I cried: "You did it for Lazarus Jesus now do it for me, raise up my baby" . . .
> (*Mitzi moves forward to embrace her, but stops abruptly at a forbidding signal from Jolie who brings her arms around in front of them, revealing the garotte in her hands.*)

                    JOLIE
Don't.
> (*Drops the garotte on the coffee-table in front of them.*)

Here's a little trinket for you two love-birds. Sit. The both of you.

MITZI
Oh, baby if you only knew, the years I've prayed—like Saint Monica—to see you again, to tell you how much I love you. Remember: "Wherever you go . . ." (*Mitzi here even starts to sing once again what she called their song, the song "Together."*) " . . . we're gonna go through it, Together . . . ."

JOLIE
SHHHhh, mother. You'll get yourself in a state. Follow Father's example. See how he sits, composed, business-like.

MITZI
But baby, compared to us you're blessed. "To never suffer cancer or the loss of a child." What we've gone through—it's foul—

JONATHAN
All these years, hounded by the press—

MITZI
Yes hounded, like dogs.

JONATHAN
Never a moment free from the glare of publicity—

MITZI
—never a moment's peace

JONATHAN
On public display, our private life held up to endless scrutiny—

MITZI
—ridicule, backbiting, innuendo—

JOLIE

But mother, it's what you always wanted. A life center stage, an endless pageant, the audience held spellbound by the spectacle of your passions. As the man said, be careful what you wish for.

JONATHAN

There's no need to take that tone with your mother. The woman has suffered—

MITZI

Oh yes if you only knew how much I've suffered. How much we've both suffered—

JOLIE

No. You haven't. You don't know what it is to suffer. That's why I'm here. To help you.

JONATHAN

Look, let's not play games. Can't we just sit and discuss this calmly, like adults?

JOLIE

Ever the pragmatist, Jonathan. By all means, let's talk. What would you like to talk about?

MITZI

(*Gushing in*) Your life, baby. Tell us about your life. Do you have a family . . . . children?

JOLIE

I never wanted children.

MITZI

(*Continuing, off in her own world*)—They're such a joy. The crown of life. But someone? Money? You must have someone, right? Someone who takes care of you?

JOLIE
No. I find solitude a great blessing. Like now, in the night when everything becomes so clear. Would you like to talk about that?

MITZI
God, baby, what about God? Does He come to you then? Cause it's when we're most alone—in the darkest night—that's when He comes.

JOLIE
God?

MITZI
Yes, God. Think how empty life is without Him ... his tender mercies ...

JOLIE
(*Suppressing response.*)

MITZI
Your father knows. Tell her, Jonathan, how dark it was before you found Him and how he came to comfort you, in your hour of need.

JOLIE
Yes, Jonathan, tell me how He came to you in your hour of need?

JONATHAN
It's true. I didn't think I could go on—after Ruth. I'd never been connected to God. But then ... in the night ... I couldn't sleep. I'd wake crying. And in my desperation, I started reading ... Reading all night. Deep books. Books like Bramblet's *The Seven Spiritual Causes of Ill Health* and yes the Bible. You have no idea what it is to read like that! All night, reading, searching, for answers to questions I'd never asked before, had no idea existed before.

JOLIE
And that's how you found Him, Jonathan—in books?

JONATHAN
Yes. I was lifted up too. Not like your mother, but in my own way. I came to understand that there's a reason for everything. That He understands all . . . forgives all. It's all part of the Plan he has for us. Like it says, not a sparrow falls. We're all part of it, see, even the least among us. And that's why good comes out of everything. Even the worst tragedies . . . like you. (*Now excited, the salesman.*) That's how it came to me . . . the idea for the Foundation—in your name—to give young girls what they need today, a firm religious and moral education—

MITZI
(*Interrupting, almost blissful*)—and its nationwide now, praise Jesus, and it's made your name, JuJu-Bee, synonymous with good works.

JOLIE
(*Ignoring Mitzi, her eyes riveted on Jonathan*) How young?

The girls. When you give them the moral values. How young?

JONATHAN
That's right. Scoff. If that's why you're here. To mock at everything we've tried to do, your mother and I, to make your life count.

MITZI
—Are you that bitter, baby? Have your own failures turned you so against life that all you can do is mock people's values?

JOLIE
No. The only thing I care about is values.

JONATHAN
Oh, and what have you done to show it? To witness your values.

JOLIE
This. I've done this.

JONATHAN
Done what, for Christ sake?

JOLIE
What it takes to get here. To be here with you now—like this.

MITZI
(*Whining*) But why did you wait so long? The years, baby, if you only knew, the years.

JOLIE
I didn't. I came as soon as I could.

JONATHAN
Why? For what perverse plan?

JOLIE
For what you both want. So we can be a family again. By facing the things families have to face. About the past, why people have children and what happens to memory over time.

JONATHAN
But it's all there. Already. The answers you seek. They're all there. In THE BOOK! (*Pause.*) The one we wrote—*The Loss of Innocence*. The explanations you seek are there!

JOLIE
I know. I read it. It was one of the longest nights of my life.
   (*Some of what follows as an inner aside.*)

I read it through—in one night—cover to cover. Searching. It hurts me to admit this but I have to. *The Loss of Innocence*. Even the title made me feel flushed, choked up. The whole time, reading, I found it hard to breathe. The prose, I grant you, is meretricious; the whole thing one long Hallmark card—

MITZI

Ohh I'm so glad. We worked so hard, on the style, to get it just right—

JONATHAN

—That's not what that word means, mother.

JOLIE

(*Continuing, oblivious of them*)—no matter. I kept turning the pages, scanning every line, the way you read a love letter . . . Or, pardon the pun, a "Dear John." How every word might contain what you seek. The reprieve. The bestowal. I read it, your book, searching . . . for myself, for the innocence the title promised. I found it all right! I should have known. That the only innocence you could mourn was your own: what you called your *naivete:* about pageants, the media, police, your friends. How *appropo*, your one flaw caught in a french word. NO! SSShhhh . . . Wait. I did . . . . I read it. Waiting. Hoping. There must be a moment, I told myself, where I'll come alive . . . me . . . a child. Now—after I'm gone, they'll find me. Know me. Create me new. Love will finally come to me from the words on a page! Words that can't possibly be fake. I was your ideal audience, the most credulous reader you'll ever find. I, who've spent my life in an abiding distrust of words, read your book as a child does, seeking a magic kingdom. But there's no child hiding in your book. SSShhh, there's something more important. A singular truth—and I found it, reading. I WAS NEVER HERE. And so my inquiry ended. I closed the book and held it—like this (*over her heart and in a gesture that is almost prayerful*) for the time it would take to accept it. But I couldn't. I opened it again, turned back, and re-read. That's how I found it—myself—in a single sentence A sentence I must have skimmed over before, when I was looking for the wrong thing. I wrote it out. I carry it with me. Here. (*Opens purse and removes piece of paper.*) I want you to read it. "Together."

JONATHAN
Whatever. Just so we can be done with this.

JOLIE
It's in the chapter about how I got into the pageants. (*Mimicking tabloids*) "Inquiring minds want to know." "How did she learn to do THAT?" Where did she get those *TALENTS?* Everything turns on the answer you give—and you know it. And try as you will to deflect it, the question isn't (*here quoting from memory lines from their book*) about my "gusto" and "my infectious smile." It's about my other talents. And so you give the answer you must. Read it. I'll be your prompter.
    (*Now reading directly from their book, which she has taken up from coffee-table.*)

"Where did she learn to do that?" Come on. I'll give you the first line. "The truth is she didn't learn it . . ."
    (*Hands book to them. Holds pause until they reluctantly comply and read together the following line.*)

JONATHAN AND MITZI
"It just came from within."

JOLIE
"It just came from within." Like you, Jonathan, I've been a reader. All my life. It's the saddest sentence I know. And the coldest. There's no child in your book. But there is a whore.

MITZI
You've no mercy. I always said it. Snippy—with no mercy.

JOLIE
Au contraire, mother. This is a mission of mercy.

JONATHAN
Then get on with it. With whatever you must do to relieve your burdens.

JOLIE

Not mine, Jonathan. Yours. The dream. The one you have every night. The one He can't take away. I'm here to help you. To wash away your tears. All you have to do is come with me—back into the dream. Remember, the vast, frozen landscape—all white. You tread in circles—shuddering—lost. You wrap your arms about you—yes, like that (*indicating actions Jonathan performs*) trying to warm yourself, but they only make you colder. And so you cut into your own chest, to wrap yourself within yourself, the way people lost in a snow storm wrap themselves within the carcass of an animal. But your blood is ice and it hangs above you as you lie there, caked in ice, the way water does from a spigot, in that interminable delay, before it drops, drops straight down, into you, into your soul. And now you see it, your own fist outside banging on the ice that encases you, trying to make a crack in it. But nothing comes back, nothing but a dry, hollow sound. And you hear it now, with each drop, the hollow sound reverberating down the endless corridors in which you wake already fleeing the other sound, the one you couldn't get enough of back then—remember—the sound I made when you held me nightly, unspeakably in your arms.

JONATHAN

And you, Jolie? Your meanness of spirit. You didn't learn that from me.

JOLIE

No. What I learned from you, Jonathan, is how to tell the truth. So say it. Say it, and we're done. Finish the sentence. 'Because after Ruth died . . . ' Say it.

(*Long pause. But he can't. He won't. She does.*)

'After Ruth died . . . . YOUR INNOCENCE BECAME A TORTURE TO ME.' That's it, isn't it?

JONATHAN

(*As it hits home, the full shock of recognition*) Nothing. Not a shred .... dignity ... pity .... nothing. Can't you leave me a shred?

JOLIE
I leave you with more. I leave you with yourself.
   (*Before he can say anything she has already turned her back on him. And is facing Mitzi. Jonathan sits silent, broken, throughout the ensuing scene.*)

Stop wringing your hands mother. (*Indicating mirror, before which Mitzi now sits, facing audience*) It's time to prepare your face. They'll be here soon and you're not ready. Here, let me help. I know how. I used to watch, when I was a child, through the door you always kept ajar. You didn't know I was there. No. That's wrong. You knew, didn't you? That I was there waiting, before dawn, to see you, barely awake, before your mirror.
   (*At beginning Mitzi sits and stares as if "composing" herself. In trance-state she is back on that morning in 1996, the 911 call to report her dead daughter kidnapped not yet made. In what follows, Jolie begins "massaging" the face the way a sculptor does clay. All the actions she performs on the face in what follows must be done with restraint, simplicity, and self-control. No urgency. Her actions the followings of an inner necessity, of one simple yet merciless step after another.*)

Where do you begin now, mother? Do you first rub off the face you put on just before sleep, cause they could come any time now, and you must be ready? Or do you just plaster one layer atop another, like a film running in reverse as you dream yourself back into your first world?

Ahh, yes, and when you get it right does your hand stray now, as it did then, across your breasts and down ...
   (*Mitzi in revery, acts out the actions Jolie describes.*)

... to rub there with the one hand while with the other you caress your face in the mirror with unguents, creams, and oils? Until you stop, as you always did, alarmed—with that stare, like there's something in the mirror you're afraid of. Then just the arm, up and down, faster and harder, your eyes darting about, the mouth open and twisted, and with your finger pointing like that, like that famous picture from your first TV appearance. Until I'd hear it : that little yelp—the fraction of a second—

But after, ahh mother, after. Your face, beautiful and serene to the finishing touches. Your eyes misty, aglow as you promenade down the aisle in Atlantic City to breathless adoration.

Breathless.
(Jolie has trouble breathing; then continues.)

But you can't stop now, can you? The hands must be forever busy. Here, where it shows through, in spite of all your arts. The lips tight, pursed: your niggardly heart come to embrace you. And the mouth, always down in a scowl now, isn't it? Your settled distaste for life. Paint an inch thick, nothing can bring it back—that smile that launched a thousand pageants.
(Mitzi now weeping, her tears adding to the portrait.)

Nothing we can do now to settle the cheekbones high and trace that hollow beneath. Nothing now but cracks and gashes running from the eyes right down into the neck, as if the thumb of a rude sculptor finally got it right and left it like that—your cruelty carved into your flesh, a cubist masterpiece, collapsing in on itself. Rouge only makes it more garish now. And your tears run mud.
(Mitzi in panic raises hands to the side of her head, as if to contain an inner pressure about to burst.)

Yes, the wigs? One of them? Maybe?
(Mitzi affixes one of the wigs from her dressing table. But before she can comb it Jolie removes her hands.)

No. Let it stay there like that, all ratted and teased like some schoolgirl who's trying to be sexy for the first time. Because this is the moment, isn't it, when it all floats before you, as in a dream, your hair like snakes so that you want to scream and run out into the street—
(Jolie raises her hands and seems about to take her fingers and rake them across Mitzi's face, the rage she has contained about to break loose. But she then reclaims herself.)

No. Not me. Here, let me brush this for you. Ahhh, to no avail, for you always come to the eyes. To these.
(During following Jolie lifts the various contact lenses that Mitzi was putting on and taking off at the beginning of this Act. She looks at each. Then at end drops all into waste-basket. Mitzi now stares, frozen, straight at the audience.)

Beautiful: Sky Blue. Hazel. Gold, and—how dare you—Green. Disposable, as advertised! None work, mother, because there's nothing left in your eyes to catch the light and reflect it. And now you see it too—don't you?—in the flicker as you try to bat then close them in that way you did so well back then. But you can't. They're lidless. And they stare now at only the one thing. Flesh. Flesh that finally falls away, crumbles in on itself and fades. Everything fades. Nothing remains but the two empty sockets. And that's when you see yourself, mother. Not shrieking. Not weeping. Not tearing at your hair. But this—a skull, hollow and grinning.

You're ready now, mother. An American Beauty Rose. Ready for the stroll down the aisle to final curtain.
(She now "lifts" the broken Mitzi and leads her across the stage to Jonathan. She joins their hands and seats them together on the couch.)

Father and mother. Man and wife. One flesh. "Together."

(*Now as the Bradys sit there, paralyzed, Jolie sutures the film back together and re-starts the projector. The video of the child performing resumes. As the lights begin to dim the adult Jolie walks straight through that image and out the door that has appeared on the back wall of the inner stage—the Door to Summer. The audience is left in the dark with the Bradys watching the film of the child performing. It plays on, but with no sound.*)

NO CURTAIN

BIBLIOGRAPHY

BOOKS:

Ramsey, John and Patsy. *The Death of Innocence.* Thomas Nelson Publishers, 2000.
Schiller, Lawrence. *Perfect Murder, Perfect Town.* Harper Collins, 1999.
Singular, Stephen. *Presumed Guilty.* New Millenium Press, 1999.
Thomas, Steve. *JonBenét: Inside the Ramsey Murder Investigation.* St. martin's Press, 2000.
Hodges, Andrew G. *A Mother Gone Bad.* Village House Publishers, 1998.
Wecht, Cyril H. and Bosworth, Charles Jr. *Who Killed JonBenét Ramsey: A Leading Forensic Expert Uncovers the Shocking Facts.* Signet/New American Library, 1998.
Smith, Carlton. *Death of a Little Princess.* St. Martin's Press, 1997.

DOCUMENTARIES:

The Case of JonBenét: The Media vs. the Ramseys, A&E, 1998
Barbara Walters Special Hour-Long Interview of John and Patsy Ramsey," *ABC,* 2000.
Painted Babies (Documentary on Child Beauty Pageants) *The Learning Channel,* 2000.
Dan Rather 48 Hours Special, *CBS,* 1998.
Katie Couric Special Hour-Long Interview with Lou Smit, *NBC,* 2001.

THERE IS ANOTHER COURT

What is all Literature next to the death of a child?
                                        Jean-Paul Sartre

Do roses know their thorns hurt?
        JonBenét Ramsey, aged 5, to family gardener

It'll never see the inside of a Court room.
                                    Detective Steve Thomas

1.

In 1997, the year after the death of JonBenét Ramsey 3,000 child beauty pageants were held in the United States. By 2001 the number of pageants held annually had grown to 25,000.

2.

The autopsy performed on JonBenét Ramsey revealed that she was sexually assaulted at the time of her death. The autopsy also found evidence of sexual abuse (digital) in the days preceding her death and chronically in the months preceding it.[1]

Unusual in such cases, the crime scene indicated that great care had been taken to wrap the body in a blanket and to place with it a favored pink nightgown.

Autopsy evidence also indicated that the murder was unusually brutal. The child was strangled by a garotte fashioned from a cord and a paint brush, but when she was in the agonal stages of death a blunt blow of extreme force was delivered to her skull. The force of this blow was such that the autopsy revealed near the back of her head a displaced section of skull about three/fourths by one/half inch.

3.

The following concluded an editorial on the murder of JonBenét Ramsey that appeared in TIME magazine on Jan 14,1997: " . . . there is the question of whether this is a work of the darkest evil imaginable or a more or less random act of malice and greed gone awry. Evil on this scale is impossible to comprehend. To know who murdered JonBenét Ramsey is to know what world we live in, where we are."[2]

4.

Lead investigator Detective Steve Thomas, after a three year investigation, obtained from the F.B.I. Crime lab the judgment that sufficient evidence had been gathered to warrant a probable cause indictment of Patsy Ramsey for JonBenét's murder. Despite an exhaustive knowledge of the facts, when it comes to offering a scenario reconstructing the crime and its motives, Thomas makes no mention of the sexual. The murder, he suggests, was the accidental result of a blow struck in rage by Patsy over JonBenét's continued bed-wetting.[3]

Detective Lou Smit, on the other hand, in an attempt to exonerate the Ramseys dwells on the sexual aspects of the case since this provides for him compelling "evidence" that an intruder must have committed the crime. Armed with the assurance that "no mother could do a thing like that"—especially not the good Christians he knows the Ramseys to be, having prayed with them—Smit seeks out "facts" sufficient to conjure a scenario peopled by a vast ring of sexual predators itching to prey on the American family. For as Smits never tires of reiterating, "JonBenét was a pedophiles dream."[4] What he never asks is how she got to be that way.

5.

Thomas and Smit's positions typify the two views that have been developed of the crime by investigators.[5] They also illustrate the force of a curious disjunctive syllogism. To put it crudely: if the mother did it the sexual must be eliminated. If the sexual is retained, the murderer must be sought outside the family. Investigation succumbs to repression. Even though two facts are presumably well known by law enforcement personnel: (1) over 80% of children sexually abused are abused by a parent or close relative; (2) 1 in 4 women and 1 in 7 men are subjected to sexual abuse in their childhood. In short, there's another possible story here and it has not been told.

6.

The repression of that story also characterizes the trajectory of how the Ramsey case has been handled in the media. Three phases can be discerned.

Phase 1: The solicitation of the audience's voyeurism. The sexuality of the videos is foregrounded and exhibited at every opportunity in the coverage of the case. A feeding frenzy for videos of JonBenét performing, the more provocative the better. The media knew that it had in the videos a rorscharch to the perverse imaginary. Sex and the child was on display in a way sure to capture a huge audience. Crassly and sensationalistically, something heartbreaking was turned into a dirty joke. The wedding of kiddie porn and necrophila. Hints and innuendoes invited viewers to project whatever their psyches desire.

Phase 2: By 1998 there is a dramatic shift in media coverage. One of the best examples: in the Rikki Kleimann special for Court TV, a panel of experts (the most cogent among them one Mark Furhmann) discuss the evidence in terms of four potential suspects:

John, Patsy, Burke (the Ramsey's son), and an intruder. Everyone is serious, objective, impartial in paying attention to what forensic evidence reveals. But all reference to the sexual is scrupulously avoided. It is as if anything connected with that topic has proven to be of no evidentiary significance and so is now off limits. And yet every six or eight minutes, with the break for a commercial, we get for approximately 20 seconds a clip from one of the more provocative JonBenét videos. The producers know, this is the hook that keeps us from switching channels. It is now, however, something that cannot be discussed.

Dan Rather exemplifies the next step in what is, we'll see, a necessary process. Reviewing the inconclusive state of investigations in the case. Rather concludes a 48HOURS special by offering his audience what amounts to moral instruction. "And then there are those videos *which some people unfortunately find provocative*."[6] But not certainly good people like us who know that Rather is telling us what we must now proclaim in order to assure our membership in the society of those with clean minds. The transformation is complete. The Ramsey case is now a pure "whodunit" having nothing to do with sex or child beauty pageants. Sex is all in the eye of the aberrant viewer. Not, assuredly, in the media. Nor in the family.

Phase 3: It can only return, accordingly, as an evil outside the family that preys on its innocence. The stage is set for Lou Smit, whose hour-long interview with Katie Couric in 2001 assures us of two things: that there are sexual predators out there, everywhere; but not in the family which is a haven of Christian and maternal love. (This interview typifies the way the Ramsey case is now handled in a media intent, in the name of fairness, on airing shows devoted to presenting "evidence" suggesting the possible innocence of the Ramseys.) A new audience is hailed by Smit: an audience appalled by sexual deviancy and ardent in sharing Smit's view of family values etc.

From these examples a clear structure can be discerned. The media solicits voyeurism. Denies that fact. Then moralistically instructs us to deny any interest in the sexual while projecting it as an evil that preys on us from outside. Voyeurism. Denial.

Projection. What we first were invited to experience as pervert we can now abjure as hysteric.

One of the ironies in this scenario is that it could have been scripted by Patsy Ramsey: who told us that the pageants "were just a Sunday thing," not a family obsession; that there is absolutely nothing sexual in them, except to those who view the innocent play of children with dirty minds; and who within a week of her daughter's death went on national TV (*Larry King Live*) to warn us: "Keep your babies close to you. There's someone out there."[7]

And so with respect to child beauty pageants and what they might reveal about the American family and American society, a discourse that should have taken place did not because the image that could have informed that discourse was rendered undecidable, yet another *aporia* of perception. Some viewers find the pageants objectionable. Others see them as good, clean fun. And then there are those few out there who "unfortunately find them provocative." They are left with the burden of their deviance. But we've been cleansed. It's all a matter of taste and opinion. The image that originally held our attention is banished lest it trouble our conscience.[8] The pleasures derived from JonBenét are locked in the eye of the beholder, but what she could have taught us remains, like our collective hearts, a blank slate. Voyeurism gave her 15 minutes of posthumous fame; she was then discarded on the dungheap of what we must forget so that cleansed of any possible knowledge we can rush to the next spectacle the media provides eager to repeat the pleasure we gain from forgetting.

Thanks to the ministrations of the media, a story that can't be told—a story about sex in the family—vanishes with the passing of the image that first made it possible to take up the emotional burden required to tell that story.

7.

And so pause, come with me now, and try to remember, if only for a moment, what you felt the first time you saw a video of JonBenét performing and learned perhaps for the first time, as I did, about child beauty pageants. Did that image enter your consciousness as enticement to voyeuristic imaginings? Were you indifferent to it? Or, perhaps, if only for a few passing moments, something else happened. Something traumatic entered your consciousness—and something broke inside you. *How could someone do this to a child?* An irrelevant question, involving a subjective judgment or the key to understanding two things. First, that a crime had been committed against JonBenét Ramsey long before her death; from which inferences followed that would knit together the salient facts about the case as they emerged. Second, that audiences would need to displace the anxiety of those inferences by appropriating the image of JonBenét voyeuristically, seeking outside the family for its explanation, or banishing it altogether as something distasteful and of no concern to decent, healthy people. Necessary defenses for otherwise her image—the image of a little girl transformed by heavy make-up to look like a Hollywood starlet, dressed in a skimpy and glittering costume, performing in calculatedly provocative gestures—stays raw in a consciousness called by that image to a painful, perhaps impossible, task: to internalize what it would be like to be her, to imagine the psyche of a child experiencing what Rilke alone perhaps has fathomed:

> Who shows a child as he [she] really is? Who sets him [her]
> in his [her] constellation and puts the measuring-rod
> of distance in his [her] hand? Who makes his [her] death
> out of gray bread, which hardens—or leaves it there
> inside his [her] round mouth, jagged as the core
> of a sweet apple? . . . . Murderers are easy
> to understand. But this: that one can contain
> death, the whole of death, even before
> life has begun, can hold it to one's heart
> gently, and not refuse to go on living,
> is inexpressible.[9]

Murderers are easy to understand—and their story conveniently displaces the one we are afraid to tell. About soul murder. About the ways, in childhood, we sacrifice ourselves to our parent's desires—and thus die within. About how the heart is broken in childhood and the psyche scarred for life. And, above all, about the child's knowledge of what is done to them—and the nature of that knowledge. To tell that story is to experience again the anxiety of who one was when to feel was to know and in one's feelings to act directly upon one's heart in primary and unalterable ways.

Can one recapture that way of being and use it to tell her story? That question involves a prior question that was brought home to us the first time we saw her image: when do we get to know what we knew then? When and how can what we felt when we saw the videos of JonBenét become a legitimate source of knowledge, a valid participant in the many "discourses" to which her story gave birth? And if the answer to that question is never....

8.
Fact, Interpretation, Narrative, Desire

What have such reflections to do with sober investigation? More than one imagines. But to tell that story we must return to Detectives Thomas and Smit.

An epistemological preliminary. The easiest conclusion to reach from the Smit/Thomas debate is the quintessentially postmodern one. As Nietzsche proclaimed, "there are no facts, only interpretations." Gather a vast body of data, as now exists on the Ramsey case. Lacking a hypothesis none of that data makes any sense. For data doesn't interpret itself: it receives significance only when we bring a hypothesis to it. Once a hypothesis is in place, certain facts emerge as unusually cogent. Others recede. And some are uncovered for the first time. That is because a hypothesis gives us a way to look and thereby to discover. A detective arrived on a scene is not a hyperempiricist awash in facts that contain infallible signs which interpret themselves. He's an interpreter actively engaged in selecting, arranging, and discovering what is "there" only if he is able to construct an account that will explain both its presence and its salience. All this maintains due to a single condition. A detective is essentially a storyteller. The ability to see patterns of significance in a body of data is not a function of objective detachment but of narrative competence.

Irony defines the dominant postmodernist response to this situation. There is and can be no end to the conflict of interpretations. Multiple accounts, each consistent unto themselves and opposed to one another, are unavoidable. We must abandon our hope for a single convincing account in favor of the endless play of competing interpretations and the superior joy that comes to those who are demystified and thus able to see each interpretation as a product of arbitrary assumptions imposed on data to arrest what would otherwise be a world lacking order, certitude, and interpretive closure. In cases like the Ramsey case where there is no single incorrigible fact—such as DNA evidence in the Simpson case—any conclusions will be a function of inferences made from a body of facts that permit other explanations which derive from a teller's ability to use those facts to tell a different story.

An aside. In such cases the method of multiple working hypotheses, to which all investigators implicitly pledge allegiance, offers no way out of the interpretive dilemma. That method, which underlies the physical sciences and which grants validity to the hypothesis that is hardest to *disprove,* depends for its possibility on conditions that do not exist in such cases as this. For here there is no single body of facts to which all hypotheses must conform. Facts are the distinct creatures of distinct hypotheses. What one investigator sees the other ignores; what is peripheral to one interpretation is central to another. The kind of story one tells is the source both of the primary data and its significance. *Rashomon* is condition general. In the legal system this condition is exploited cynically, attorneys fashioning opposed stories that succeed not because they are backed by evidence that proves something "beyond a reasonable doubt" but because a jury finds one account—usually the simplest one—more appealing. But detectives Smit and Thomas are also bound to it, as are we all, though for reasons we have barely begun to investigate.

This view summarized in this section is regarded by many as

the last word about interpretation because it so neat squares with central postmodernist dogmas. Everything is a construct; language a game; identity, reference, and closure myths. This story suppresses another story, however, one that points toward a more disruptive and more concrete understanding of interpretation. Thanks to Smit and Thomas we are in a position to tell it.

9.

As noted before, there is a tale here that has not been told. Nor researched in any consistent and thorough way. Its possibility emerges by following what in this case is the equivalent of the advice that Deep Throat gave Bob Woodward when he told him to "follow the money." Follow the sexualization—not by displacing it from the family but by using it to track down the story that emerges when one lets that focus expand. Consider, for example, the following chronology which has thusfar eluded the attention of investigators.

(1) August 6, 1990—birth of JonBenét Patricia Ramsey. John Bennett Ramsey names his daughter after himslf. Patsy adds the inverted (sic) French accent mark.

(2) January 8, 1992—death in car crash of Beth Ramsey (18), daughter of John Ramsey from first marriage.

(3) January, 1992 and thereafter—John Ramsey, traumatized for the first time in his life, has his sleep interrupted nightly by a sort of terrible keening from which he wakes already weeping bitterly. Ramsey, a man known for the firm reign he has always had over his feelings, regresses in numerous ways. Among them the composition of poems that, according to the Ramsey's housekeeper, portray Beth as a little girl and include lines such as "And you are starting to have a woman's looks which are clear."[10]

(4) July 4, 1993—Patsy Ramsey diagnosed with stage 4 aggressive ovarian cancer.

(5) August 31, 1993 and thereafter—Patsy tells pediatrician

JonBenét has no phobias and "no problems in sexual education." Frequent nighttime bed-wetting by JonBenét continues up to time of her death, accompanied in the months preceding her death with frequent soiling.[11]

(6) 1993-1994—Patsy in remission. Claims miracle cure through prayer.

(7) Winter 1995-Spring 1996—JonBenét's work in pageants begins. Patsy procures help of a twenty-one year old former beauty queen to teach JonBenét how to increase the sexual appeal of her performance. In keeping with that intent, JonBenét's costumes become more extreme (including a feathered costume reminiscent of Sally Rand), with heavier makeup and platinum dyed hair.

(8) June 1996. Patsy tells friend she has no pleasure in sex anymore. Friend suggests she get pornographic videos and watch them with John. She doesn't.

(9) December 25-26, 1996—Death of JonBenét Ramsey.

(10) Autopsy of JonBenét Ramsey reveals sexual violation at the time of her death. Autopsy also reveals evidence of recent abuse (digital) in the days preceding death and vaginal tearing consistent with digital sexual abuse in the months prior to death.

Is there a story buried here?

10.

This chronology, similar to the one Faulkner provides as an appendix to *Absalom, Absalom!* suggests a narrative consistent with the large body of evidence that points to Patsy as the murderer. That story is also consistent with everything we have come to know about John and Patsy Ramsey from sources such as Lawrence Schiller's scrupulously objective *Perfect Murder, Perfect Town,* a book invaluable for the wealth of information it gives us about John and Patsy as provided by their own statements and the testimony of relatives, friends, and acquaintances. Moreover, it offers a solution to the other great mystery of the case: namely, the motives behind John Ramsey's steadfast effort to shield his wife from prosecution.

Here, in its bare bones, is that hypothetical story. Former Beauty Queen Patsy Ramsey, to reclaim her wounded narcissism, recreates herself in her daughter. For that project to succeed she does everything in her power to sexualize her child and to increase the sexual dimensions of her performance. That act has one unintended consequence. John Ramsey, traumatized by the death of his daughter Beth and sexually rejected by his wife, finds in his daughter the comfort he seeks. The narcissistic subject has become the sexual rival. In revenge Patsy kills JonBenét, the sexual violation accompanying the crime in keeping with its motive. John then helps her escape prosecution so that his own deed will remain concealed. Like Paolo and Francesca they are bound to one another forever.

This hypothesis has two things in its favor that Thomas and Smits' stories lack. It sustains the sexual as it develops in the family and connects it to the psyches of the participants. Sex is here central as are the JonBenét videos. Preserving what can be seen in them is the key that lights up everything else. A sexualized child is at the center of this tale. And sexualization is here not peripheral to this family but points inward—to its conflicted core. The focus on the sexual enables us to construct a narrative that preserves the preponderance of facts in a way that accounts for the motives and psyches of the participants. It preserves what first attracted attention to the case—a little girl made up to look like a mature woman performing a song and dance in a provocative manner—in a way that sustains the disruptive, traumatic impact of that image. It is the reality that leads us to the data and enables us to grasp in it that which is "impossible to comprehend," a story about "the darkest evil imaginable."

This hypothesis is also consistent with everything we have come to know about the character of the participants. About the extents to which a narcissistic and hysterical woman will go to exploit her child in order to fulfill her unmet needs and desires; and the tyranny with which she forces everyone in the family to comply with the demands of her psyche. About how the scars that cancer inflicted on her body-psyche, and her self-conception in terms of an image of "feminine beauty," create the need to deny that loss by projecting her lost self-image into her child. And about what can happen to a withdrawn, controlling man who has always kept emotions at a distance and who finds no way to cope when he experiences traumatic loss for the first time in his life and thrashes about clutching at anything that will relieve his panic and who in protracted mourning for his dead daughter receives little comfort from a wife preoccupied with the overblown projection of her own needs. It's a story about "the woe that is in marriage,"—the lack of communication, the mutual avoidance, the distance in times of need, and the attempt by both parents to find a compensatory relationship in the child. But above all it's a story about childhood, not as we like to picture it, an innocent field of dreams basked in the glow of unconditional love, but childhood as the place of the greatest heartbreaks, of violations that set the heart against itself. It's about the child's desperate efforts to win the parent's love and the willingness to sacrifice oneself to that quest; of the child's attempt to fill the *lack* in the parents and the inability of parents to see what the imposition of their needs does to the child. As such it is a story about the family as an institution defined by conflict and about conflict as the origin of the psyche; i.e., of psychological birth as the attempt to mediate the conflicts of and between our parents. And in all this it is a story about the centrality of the sexual to the psyche. Sex is here the key to everything. To the psychosexual conflicts that define the parents and the sexualization of a child as the place where those conflicts coalesce in wounds that define the child's psyche.

It is thus a story about the dark side of the American dream in a family that Geraldo Rivera termed "the perfect family;" a family that represents both the achievement of the dream and its insatiability; about the family's need for public display and the extents to which parents will go in using their children to pursue commodified signs that enhance their status. For the Ramseys are representative—of our collective obsessions and their cost to our children; of the hollowness of the public masks we wear and of what is beneath them. In all this, however, it is primarily about how the terrible pressures of the family create the wounded psyche of the child. For to tell this story is to focus, of necessity, on the psyche of JonBenét Ramsey and the many crimes done to her before her death. But this is a story most audiences don't want to hear. Otherwise the next time we see her image we'll feel again what we felt the first time we saw it or feel now for the first time what we should have felt then.

11.
JonBenét as Sign-System

Approached as an object through the application of the methods dear to a postmodern sensibility fascinated with the semiotic description of sign-systems, JonBenét Ramsey presents a singularly revealing "text": the perfect embodiment of the fantasmatic dream of the American patriarchy—the child-woman who represents in a coyly perverted way the view of women that permeates a culture enslaved to a pervading pedophilia. Think of the Playboy Bunny and her effort to assure the viewer that her breasts are full and her mind empty. The body may be 21 but her psyche remains prepubescent. That's what the empty, mindless expression of the "come take me any way you want me I live just to please you" look conveys. As does the smile which doesn't come from inside her but is your own dirty thought mirrored back to you as ready compliance. In the iteration of this image a single message is obsessively communicated: woman is sexual object, but never sexual threat. The perfect woman is a 25 year-old who looks and acts 16 or, better, a 16 year-old who looks and acts 25. The interchangeability is essential to the function of the image. It obliterates the possibility of psychological growth during a time period central in the development of psychosexual identity.[12] The other function of the image is equally leveling. There is no time after this image; woman is disposable the moment all can see what can no longer be air-brushed away. In the Bunny the commodification both of male and of female desire finds its objective correlative. This is what one wants to purchase; what one will purchase any cosmetic or prosthetic aid to become. Its sexual message is, of course, the key to the image. Woman is sexually available and utterly pliable—the object the male bends to the designs of whatever fantasy he chooses, in his freedom, to project. The image whispers the long desired message: "She'll do whatever you want because she's too dumb and too dependent to object." In sex woman contributes the body, man provides the mind.

What object is more fit to realize the psychological disorder underlying this fixation than a child? Especially if we can show that in the child sex is already blooming but combined with innocence and the need for adult recognition and approval. The child beauty pageant stages the patriarchal fantasy in its first realization—as if it is a fact of nature and not of culture. Little girls love to play at being grown up women—and to compete with one another to see who does it best. Their ripening into their future role is already at work in them; they already know, by nature, what it involves. Given the chance to perform every little girl will find what's already in her. Which is why the progressive sexualization of pageant performances is unstoppable. In the pageant the future sexuality of woman is on display as something that is already there, ready and willing to solicit the adult male gaze and unable to halt what that gaze provokes. It is as if in the child beauty pageant the culture has found a way to institutionalize what Humbert Humbert knew was a carefully constructed lie: the claim that little Lolita already has big ideas and will go after "Daddy" (Humbert as stepfather being Nabokov's concession to the censorious super-ego) the first chance she gets. In fact, she won't just go after Daddy she'll go down on him, this being the function of the attention paid to magnifying the size and redness of the lips as displaced vagina. And so as these child-women disport in carefully choreographed numbers the audience gets a chance to gasp with pleasure as a chorus joined in shared amazement: "why, just look at her: where did she get those talents?"[13]

And yet, as we all know, the whole thing is a masquerade.[14]

The kids are carefully coached, their numbers rehearsed down to the smallest gesture and, as Patsy knew, most successful if a "girl" with experience in "adult" pageants can be brought in to teach the child how to mimic the pouts and poses and calculated turn-ons that give the child's performance what adult pageants perforce renounce in favor of "the bathing suit competition." The whole thing is a strip-tease—a soft-core one that stops at the point Gypsy Rose Lee revealed as the key one: the point when the teased audience joins in with the approval that enables the stripper to take the next step in the infinitely deferred movement toward exposure. *Differance* made present. A strip is a wet-dream, an overture to masturbation at that later time when in the revival of the image the audience finds the aid it needs in order to reach orgasm. The elaborate feather costume Patsy chose for JonBenét for one of her last pageants showed Patsy, as usual, in a rush to outstrip the other mothers in pursuit of their common goal. That costume, a deliberate allusion to the legendary stripper Sally Rand provides an overt *index* of the mind of the mothers directing the show. The child beauty pageant is a studied play of allusions; of references in homage and imitation of the female images that haunt the American imaginary: catch the gesture toward Marilyn Monroe's great number in *How to Marry a Millionaire* as you watch a child slowly peel off her glove; the pout Bardot made famous; Natalie Wood in *Gypsy* when she first caught on to what one must do to please an audience then waxed to the role; Nancy Kwan in *Flower Drum Song*, supposedly alone in her bedroom yet dancing before the mirror the joy of "being a girl," etc. You don't have to go to *L.A. Confidental* to find "a whore cut to look like Lana Turner or Veronica Lake." All you have to do is visit a child beauty pageant to know the truth of women who have found the perfect forum to *display the conditions of an impossible and self-contradictory desire*. Womanliness as masquerade by those who can no longer fulfill the image and so in the child pay a last nostalgic visit to the shrine of one's most famous victories or seize in desperation the chance to "win" for the first time. The pageants thus present a theatre of *resentment*, of anger *projected* not toward men but toward oneself through the child who is made to re-incarnate the only thing one was ever allowed to be. Mothers here program their daughters as they were programmed by their mothers so that all will remain fixated on the role that assures perpetual failure disguised as blushing anticipation. Hamlet's observation about the folly of the troupe of child actors "who cry out against their own succession" is here reversed. As Daisy Fay Buchanan said when told her baby was a girl: "Allright. I'm glad it's a girl. And I hope she'll be a fool. That's the best thing a girl can be in this world, a beautiful little fool."[15] In this, as in so much else, Patsy Ramsey is the representative figure. Formed by the founding mother, Nedra, to cash in on her one asset before it withers, Patsy in marrying a rich man fulfilled the common dream of the adult-former-beauty-queen. She then saw it fade away into the light of common day as she put on flesh and sought new ways to live out the perpetual hunger of her station. Cancer then ravaged the only identity she ever had. Depression and hysterical denial found in the daughter, however, a way to re-live her moment of triumph while knowing what the daughter can't—that it's all evanescent and doomed to failure. In Sartrean terms, Patsy in JonBenét gets to be the impossible identical subject-object whose freedom is found in turning another into the thing one was.[16] Child beauty pageants offer such women the bliss of pseudo-transcendance: the chance to look back on themselves and enjoy manipulating the male gaze. Through the child one achieves a freedom that is one with the bad faith one projects into the child as their identity. It is, of course, a common story about mothers and daughters, but in the child beauty pageant it finds a ghostly realization, the acting out, as in a dream, of the *logic* that informs the contradictory conditions of a self-contradictory desire.

The child beauty pageant is the marriage of narcissism and fakery celebrated as talent. Talent is here the ability to display a precocious sexuality as the role one has already learned to play before one learns anything else, as the identity-formation one takes delight in as a performative that never wants to end. It's all a fake and the mothers know it. But the key to this fake is that it present itself as real. The "innocence" of the child guarantees the success of that project: the child-woman who lives only for her role; on stage before she ever gets to the stage of womanhood, the perfect performer who, in her innocence, is one with her role and fulfilled in the playing of it. In their daughters the mothers present *womanhood* as something they have created—not something that created them. Thereby they triumph over the male gaze which is here present even when absent as the subject for whom the whole thing is staged. But in offering that gaze a sexuality absent of guile, open for inspection, and fulfilled in the solicitation of male approval the mothers become the true audience competing with one another to see who has mastered the game all are fated to play. The pageants thus present a battle for pure prestige among slaves.[17]

But if the pageants realize a ghostly freedom for the mothers, they perpetuate perpetual frustration for the child. For the main thing pageants stage is the anxiety of the performer—an anxiety that can't be resolved yet must be concealed. Documentaries on the pageants make one thing clear. The children who participate in them live to please their audience—and are crestfallen whenever they fail. Here performance permits no difference (*differance*), no otherness between the performer and her act. *Performance* exists here in a way that is possible only for the child, a way that exceeds even the greatest of method actors. The self-worth of the performer is engaged without reserve. Everything depends on pleasing the audience. If love is what the child desperately needs, it is here what is at stake. Performance here reveals with an immediacy that is crushing what most women in American society learn only with time: that one's worth is determined by one's ability to play this role. The pageant thereby stages as spectacle the audience's deepest motive and need: *psychological cruelty* as the one pleasure that binds parent and child in capitalist society.

That is what gives the pageants their *raison d'etre* and their justification. (It is, in fact, the primary justification that has been advanced by pageant supporters and sponsors post-Ramsey.) They are a parable about *competition as the law and the prophets in capitalist society*. In order to produce the conditions necesssary for its own reproduction a society must produce *subjects* whose psyches are ruled by the logic that informs the society as a whole. As one of my favorite TV sports commentators frequently points out in praise of little league baseball, youth football etc.: "it's never too early to teach kids the value of competition." For that lesson to sink in there must always be "the thrill of victory" but more importantly "the agony of defeat" for only then will subjects formed by competition commit their very being to it. In the child beauty pageant the demand inflicted on young boys finds for the other sex a gendered apotheosis. Just as little boys must incessantly strive to beat one another in sports, to win at any cost, little girls from early on must display their sexuality to one another in competitions where to lose is to suffer humiliation and to internalize the feeling that there is something deeply deficient in one's "femininity." Thus we circle back to the Playboy Bunny and her crowning effort: not the posing of her body but the look on her face—the bliss of mindlessness in rapt fascination with the communication of her commodification.

And so while we loudly proclaim an ideology of unconditional love as the truth of the American family, the pageants provide a telling picture of our actual condition: that children in our culture are the slaves of parental, collective disorders.

12.
JonBenét as Subject

If one sees only the above in JonBenét one misses what makes the videos truly compelling. It is there, especially toward the end, in the dead look in the eyes and the broken, marionette-like gestures that fracture the performance from within. Something else is going on here, something not explainable in the language of semiotic sign-systems. Something in excess and in opposition. JonBenét has found a way "to signal through the flames:"[18] (1) the desperateness of the child's willingness to do anything to gain the parent's love; (2) the cost of that effort in the child's soul; and (3) an incipient protest over parental lovelessness and betrayal. JonBenét's eyes are dead because that is the only expression adequate to the hopelessness of her condition. She has found a way in *action* to synthesize the lessons taught by Brecht and Artaud. She is her own alienation-effect, the performance that puts question marks around all such performances by revealing at their foundation the *existential being of the human subject.*[19]

What JonBenét shows is that a child is more than a blank slate to be writ upon so that she will become, as sign-system, the bearer of parental desires and ideological imperatives; that human identity is not just the multiplicity of language games and social communities into which we are inserted as subjects subjected to language and thereby to socially determined meanings.[20] JonBenét remains untimely well beyond the time of her fifteen minutes of fame because she reminds us that before we are the desire of the Other we are something else: subjects existentially at issue and at risk as only a child can be. What the JonBenét videos reveal is that the child suffers what is done to it and manifests that suffering in ways that can be seen by parents and by anyone unafraid to see what stares them in the face. It is interesting, in this regard, to know that John Ramsey, speaking at his daughter's memorial, let everyone know that he did not approve of child beauty pageants. More's the pity that his avowed love and parental responsibility led to no action to protect her or to intervene on her behalf.

In the late videos JonBenét teaches all of us, as parents, what is the most valuable lesson. Children know what we do to them. They know who we are, what we want, and what our desire costs them. They know it and express their knowledge with a clarity that later falls to repression. For they know it in their *feelings*. In them feeling is *cognition*. Feeling is *being*. It is *who* one is and how one acts when affected by the other. *For it is how one acts upon oneself when the actions of the other open wounds that never heal.* All of this, of course, is what parents are quick to deny when they tell us, "don't bring up the past; the past is past;" when they assure themselves that children can't possibly understand or remember what happens to them. The image of JonBenét weighs on us like a nightmare because she shows us that the opposite is the truth. That the psyche is formed and broken in childhood; that in childhood one experiences the deepest violations and betrayals, the ones that last as permanent wounds defining the body-psyche that bears them as its identity. Such is the story psychoanalysis tried to tell about the psycho-sexual formation of children and thus perhaps the main reason why most everyone today is intent on dismissing it as *passe*. For the actual message it conveys is that there is neither repression nor recovery. When one abuses a child in their body one wounds the psyche to the core, for it is in the body that psyche is lived in the most immediate and intimate ways, ways that are engaged whenever we relate to another in love and intimacy. [See below # 23.].

This is not a story we want told. Nor one easy to tell. For to tell it one must internalize the psyche of JonBenét and make her psyche the subject of one's tale. The hardest thing is not to fathom the psyches of Patsy and John. "Murderers are easy to understand." All one needs is an advanced understanding of the psychodynamics of cruelty—an understanding of how discontent with oneself works like an ulcer in the soul. To understand JonBenét Ramsey is to take up the greater and far more painful task: *to abide within the space of trauma and find there the terms for a tragic understanding.*

Such a story can't be told we are told because it poses too great a threat to the reader.[21] To tell her tale violates the implied contract that unites narrators to readers: the contract that the reader's emotional needs will be uppermost and that anything that would prove too great a shock to that system will be contained through narration so that what would otherwise cause inordinate and meaningless pain will be made manageable, subjected to the transformations needed to adapt it to our psyche and its needs. [See below, #19.] To understand the implications of these reflections we must turn again to Thomas and Smit.

13.

Thomas and Smit provide two representative examples of what happens when a narrator is not up to the demands of the subject. Steve Thomas spent three years developing the case against

Patsy Ramsey. During that time he was, by his own account, shocked and horrified by much that he learned. While working long hours and with considerable interference from his superiors and the Ramsey's attorneys he developed a serious thyroid condition requiring permanent medication. His account of the crime and of Patsy's motives, however, offers the weakest possible construction of what happened. The violent and sexual nature of the murder drops away as does any attempt to fathom the psyche of the perpetrator. There is, in fact, little if any psychology in Thomas' account. The murder is an accident committed in a fit of almost understandable parental rage over bedwetting. Thomas may have known that he was beyond the capacities of both head and heart in trying to tell a story consistent with the data. He also may have anticipated the revulsion and incredulity that would greet such a tale. He may even, cagily, have been offering Patsy a chance to plead to a lesser charge; though he could not have known the glee of Lin Wood, the Ramsey's attorney, at the prospect of suing Thomas, using the very data Thomas collected about the grisly and sexual nature of the crime to invalidate the limp account of circumstance and motive that Thomas provides. Whatever the reasons, in place of the story he was unable to tell Thomas substituted a story more acceptable to audiences who find they can accommodate the belief that an overwrought parent can accidentally kill their child but not that a mother could act, consistent with the data, in a way that impels us to contemplate "the darkest evil imaginable."

For Lou Smit, on the other hand, dwelling on the horrors of the crime provides the rationale that exonerates the parents. It does so because Smit (unlike Thomas) brings to his tale a tidy, homespun psychology fashioned from the ideologically favored American pieties about mothers, the family, and what we know for sure about god-fearing Christians who attend Church regularly and are acknowledged as upstanding members of the community. No mother, Smits tells us, could do what was done to JonBenét Ramsey. Armed with that assurance he seeks out—and invents— "evidence" that will support his cause. Not surprisingly, he finds things, which no one has noticed before (the possibility of a stungun), that lead to conjectures which cannot be confirmed and other "facts" that cannot be dated temporally and that thus lacks both the evidentiary significance and the sinister meaning Smit ascribes to them.[22] They are sufficient, however, for another purpose. They sustain a narrative that is free to conjure the image of a vast network of pornographers and pedophiles—remember "JonBenét was a pedophiles dream"—who prey on the family from outside. "Unimaginable evil" can be sustained in Smit's narrative because it has been rendered melodramatic and placed in a realm securely removed from the world of the audience. One doesn't have to suffer the horror of infanticide or parental sexual abuse; nor confront, as a result, thoughts that challenge the ideological commonplaces essential to Smit's reasoning.

Both tellers, in short, have found a way to protect themselves and their audience from what is too painful to bear. The irony of their debate is their agreement on one thing: *no mother could do what the evidence shows was done to JonBenét.* They concur in this, however, not because the evidence warrants it but because for both narrators certain emotional needs must be satisfied and other emotions exorcised. Both tellers, in short, lack the psychological competence and emotional fortitude needed to sustain a traumatic awareness.

These factors are the ones that ultimately prove determinative in interpretation. That is why even the most compelling "evidence" can always support an explanation diametrically opposed to the conclusion to which the evidence points. Consider a final, telling example. As previously noted, great care was taken in clothing the dead child and putting a favored pink nightgown next to her. Such postmortem care is usually a sign that the murderer was close to and cared about the child. Not long after this point was raised, however, one of the investigators in the Boulder D.A.'s office saw in this evidence confirmation of another hypothesis: a killer of unbelievable cunning created this display to delude investigators.[23] When *possibility* is bound only by imagination there is no way that "evidence" can be anything but the spur to desire.

The predictable postmodern response to this situation—the

celebration of relativism, multiple incompatible accounts, and irony is an attempt to short-circuit a more difficult and more concrete task: the understanding and the critique of narratives in terms of the psychological motives and emotional needs that they fulfill. In some cases a tragic, traumatic tale is alone adequate to the "facts," no matter how great the violence such a tale does to our emotional and psychological needs. (An aside. This is, I think, the true achievement of Faulkner's *Absalom, Absalom!,* which is often seen as the model of ironic, multiple narration. The tragic understanding that Quentin and Shreve move toward in a cold room in Harvard in 1909 is alone adequate to the totality of facts that are the only record we have of what happened in 1860-1865 to those who perished long before those who tell their tale were born.)

To tell a tragic tale about JonBenét Ramsey, however, extends our capacities to the breaking point. "Unspeakable evil" here inhabits the same domestic space we do and activates strong resistance because it whispers to us things we don't want to hear. It is a tale that has not been told not because their isn't a preponderance of evidence to support it, but because no one has brought to that evidence the psychological competence and tragic readiness required to endure the emotions that tale opens in the psyche. The task before the teller of such a tale is not only to understand the darkness of two adult psyches but to focus that darkness on the horror of what is done to the psyche and body of a child. Sustaining such a tale requires a narrator who would possess two things that Thomas and Smit and their putative audiences lack. First, an ability to probe in depth the psychosexual conflicts of human identity and the ways in which those conflicts inform the actions of the adult protagonists in this tale. Second, the ability to sustain the traumatic emotions that erupt when one focuses that knowledge on the terrible things done to a child; that is, when one sees JonBenét as a person and not as an object and tries to understand things from her point of view. None of Smit's pieties are any longer viable; none of Thomas' attempts to deflect the horror avail. Aristotle claimed that the bare facts of a tragic tale were sufficient to create tragic emotions. What he should have added: that is why so few audiences are willing to hear such things and to sustain the anxieties and emotions they unleash. For JonBenét Ramsey's story asks us to become aware of the family in a way that really counts. A way adequate to statistics such as these: current data indicates that in America 1 in 4 females and 1 in 7 seven males are sexually abused in their childhood; and that in over 80% of cases the abuser is a parent or relative. This, the story that could have been JonBenét's legacy and the only fitting response to the pleasures a mass audience derived from her fate, remains untold.

14.

The dread of confronting the implications of such data is the reason behind the many deflections that have characterized the Ramsey investigation. Let me cite a conspicuous example which bears directly on the scenario outlined in numbers 9 and 10. Boulder investigators were interested in the possibility of uncovering evidence that might support the hypothesis that John Ramsey sexually abused his daughter. The method they used to investigate this question and reach what they regarded as a firm conclusion is a comic monument to the ability to displace what stares one in the face. Investigators interviewed Ramsey's first wife, his children from his first marriage, and acquaintances from this period and found no evidence of sexual abuse. Pedophiles are born, not made they reasoned and armed with that assumption they were able to dispose of three important considerations, one conceptual, two empirical. Sexual dysfunctions often follow a traumatic event. The absence of aberrant behavior in the past is no assurance regarding the future. John Ramsey never experienced traumatic loss before the death of his daughter Beth. And by all accounts he was unprepared for the profound regressions that came in the wake of that loss. Moreover, his second marriage presented two circumstances lacking from his first: (1) Patsy, the Beauty queen, and the hothouse sexual atmosphere diffused by her hysteric behaviors coupled with her avoidance of sex with John and (2) JonBenét, the beloved daughter, transformed before his eyes into a sexual object trained to perform in provocative and seductive manners. But attending to such matters would have focused investigators on what was before them, obviating investigations such as the one launched to visit every place in Boulder where pornographic videos are rented to see if John was ever a customer. (That investigation was nothing to the subsequent investigation, at the demand of the Ramsey's attorneys, into every sex offender in Boulder and into any other group or individual the Ramseys deemed worthy of investigation.[24] What we have here is not scientific devotion to the method of multiple working hypotheses but its parody, a parody necessitated by the need to deflect awareness from what one must try to fathom if one sticks with the primary data. Final proof of this point is provided by the failure of investigators to undertake any inquiry into Patsy's past with respect to this issue. The apparent assumption of investigators was that no such inquiry was necessary since women do not sexually abuse their female children. Another painful idea was thereby deflected thanks to a convenient lack of psychological knowledge. The investigators remained blissfully unaware of what any good Social Service professional could have told them and which is well documented in books such as *The Last Secret: Daughters Sexually Abused by Mothers*.[25] Vincible ignorance absolved them of the need to trouble their psyches with such knowledge.

15.

But investigators alone are powerless to dispose of all the anxieties raised by the Ramsey case. Other agencies are needed. Such is the task that falls to reporters and commentators who supply the ideological reminders needed to put the heart and mind to rest. Let me cite only the most conspicuous example, which bears directly on the scenario outlined in numbers 9 and 10. If Patsy did it, why has John done everything in his power to help her escape prosecution for the murder of a child who, by all accounts, he deeply loved? That question is troubling because, like the JonBenét videos, it points, in unsettling ways, toward the tangled web that is the family. What did Patsy have on John that would compel his support? Lest we remain vexed by that question, Lawrence Schiller toward the end of a book scrupulous in its effort to avoid conclusions about anything, even the most mundane matters, assures us that we can be sure of one thing: neither Patsy nor John ever asked the other if he or she were the murderer.[26] Such assurance defies common sense, legal strategy, and all we know about these particular agents. Are we to imagine this question as one that never arose for either? Or once awake did it succumb to repression and the implicit faith of a perfect love? Imagine Patsy bearing such a question in silence? Or John, an intelligent and scrupulous man, remaining oblivious to the preponderance of evidence implicating his wife? The assurance Schiller offers is inviting, however, because it gives his audience a way to exorcise a troubling spectre, that of the parents in cahoots, one the killer of their child, the other compelled to protect that killer. For that image leaves us with painful thoughts about the family and what transpires there.

16.

All such deflections are nothing, however, to the final absolution Schiller offers when he concludes his book by reminding us that it is our moral duty to presume the Ramseys innocent until they are proven guilty in a Court of Law.[27] We are instructed, in effect, to wait for Godot because as anyone who has followed this case knows, and as Steve Thomas ruefully remarks, "it'll never see the inside of a courtroom." For three reasons: (1) the massive bungling by the Boulder police, including contamination of the crime scene, in the initial collection of evidence; (2) the politics of the Boulder District Attorney's office and its unwillingness (i.e., O.J. fallout) to prosecute the case unless assured of "a slam dunk;" and (3) the skill of the Ramsey's attorneys and media consultants in exploiting numbers one and two in order to intimidate Boulder authorities and investigators. Be that as it may, most readers I suspect accept Schiller's admonition for two reasons. First, because it corresponds to the dominant ideology of our time: the reduction of the being of the human subject to one's legal-juridical identity with the resulting assumption that the legal system provides the only forum for reasoning about and reaching legitimate conclusions about the many questions raised by an event such as the murder of JonBenét Ramsey.[28] Second, because it gives us a way to wash our hands of JonBenét—and feel moralistic for doing so. Like a good Derridean, perpetual deferral cleanses us of the motives that fed public fascination with the case. Everything traumatic connected with her image accordingly recedes in Hobbesian memory—i.e., "memory is decaying sensation"—as we proclaim our fealty to the Law and our willingness to acquiesce in the limits it places on understanding.

17.
There is Another Court

There's only one thing wrong with this argument. It doesn't have the backing of the Court, which holds a far subtler position; one that calls in cases such as this one not for an end to discussion but for the social and moral necessity of a discussion of another kind. That discourse requires the convening of another Court where another kind of deliberation takes place and another kind of knowledge is attained. Often cases that raise issues of great public concern find no resolution in the legal system. It is then, the Court holds, the duty of other public forums to offer other ways of reaching warranted conclusions about such issues. Such, the Court contends, is the social function of literary representation. See, for example, *Street v. National Broadcasting Co.*, and *Davis v. Costa-Gavras*. Moreover, such forums employ ways of knowing and canons of evidence that have little or no standing within the self-imposed limits of the legal system. The Court, in short, recognizes the duty of culture to *supplement* it and calls on the cognitive powers of works of art to provide a knowledge that is different from what can be attained legally yet binding in another and deeper way. In realizing its limits and its *aporias* the legal system gives the cultural a social and ethical mandate. The Court thus holds a more serious view of the arts than the arts for the most part hold of themselves. Literature is that public forum in which we try to reach warranted knowledge about events that the legal system has found itself powerless to resolve and which it acknowledges as all the more pressing by reason of that inability.

Before that Court can go into session, however, a final legal matter needs to be resolved. A common assumption holds that any discussion or representation of the Ramsey case that would charge either parent with the crime is open to prosecution for libel. Such, however, is not the case, as a knowledge of the Law reveals. When, through their actions, people "voluntarily inject themselves into a particular public controversy" and assume "a role of prominence ... in order to influence its outcome (*see 50 Am. Jur.2d Libel and Slander* and *Foretich v. Capital Cities/ABC*,)" those individuals make themselves *public figures* and therefore cannot later assert the claims of *private citizens* with respect to representations of them that they find objectionable. This is the fortunate and unintended consequence of the strategy pursued by the Ramseys and their lawyers in an attempt to influence the media, shape public opinion, and intimidate investigators through a steady stream of TV appearances and other public activities. Examples include the Ramseys appearance on commercial television shows such as *Larry King Live* and a Barbara Walters *20/20* special; their active participation in the production of a British documentary shown in the United States on *A&E* and titled *The Case of JonBenét: The Media vs. the Ramseys*; the publication and promotion of their book *The Death of Innocence*; and the continuing media events, labeled press conferences, arranged for them by their attorneys and media consultants. The success of this strategy in intimidating the Boulder legal authorities has its ironic corollary. Thanks to John and Patsy, the other Court is given the warrant to prosecute its duties free of restraint. (This does not, however, prevent the general audience, and, as I've learned, many professionals in the arts, from raising the libel flag when it comes to what this Court must do in giving the Ramseys the representation they so richly deserve. The libel flag is convenient, however, because it provides another easy way to dispose of JonBenét.)

18.

"It is not the function of the poet to relate what has happened, but what may happen—what is possible, according to the law of probability. Poetry, therefore, is more philosophical than history." Aristotle, *The Poetics*.

As its first theorist Aristotle realized, the other Court, which was founded by Aeschylus in the *Oresteia*, is not a Court of the possible but of the probable, with the latter determined not by empirical but by exacting psychological criteria. The task of this Court, when dealing with traumatic events, is to search into the depths of the human psyche in an effort to fathom the terrible reasons behind the terrible things we do to one another. That duty, consistent with the kind of psychological reasoning proper to this Court, requires confronting us with things we don't want to know. [See Essay 2]

We fail to understand the nature of this Court because we've lost an understanding of the distinct logic that it brings to deliberation about matters that cannot be solved in a legal-juridical framework. A Court of the probable is not devoted to the charms of the whodunit and the search to unearth the one "fact" everyone else has overlooked. Nor is it a court in which *possibility* is free to disport itself in constructing explanations bounded only by human inventiveness.[29] The Court of the probable is informed by a single canon: probable reasoning into the psychological motives that will offer the most coherent account of a body of data consistent with an understanding of the darkest places in the human psyche. This is the knowledge *Antigone, Medea, Othello, Macbeth*, etc. offer that other Courts cannot. The task of this Court is to preserve the psychological significance of the facts central to an event—the significance, for example, of what the JonBenét videos reveal—in the *unity* of a drama or narrative that *connects* all of the data by offering a depth psychological understanding of the central agents and their actions. In such inquiry psychological scrutiny is the source both of the central data to be explained and of the psychological explanation most consistent with what can be inferred from that data. And sometimes, as in the Ramsey case, such inquiry requires fathoming "the darkest evil imaginable."

Such inquiry moves from the start beyond the limits of the *genres* in which Thomas and Smit cast their tales.[30] While Thomas eschews psychology and Smits employs one based on sentiment rather than insight, probable reasoning when faced with traumatic events requires the full exercise of what may be termed *the tragic sensibility*. That sensibility is ruled by a single canon: one must sustain the traumatic dimensions of a subject against all efforts to flee or deny them. Probable reasoning about the deep conflicts that define the psyche is the entry of the tragic poet into events. Tragic reasoning is the ability to preserve those facts we are reluctant to confront because of the pain they involve and connect them with other facts that escape detection because they would extend and magnify that pain. Preserving the traumatic is here one's way to a unifying understanding. To gain it the tragic poet knits trauma into trauma in an attempt to fathom the full dimensions of a single tragic action.

As the tragic poets show, most of the beliefs and ideologies that constitute normalcy are of no avail when dealing with tragic events. Such events are beyond the scope of the comforting beliefs that compose what most people call *human nature*. Tragic understanding only comes to those who can strip away the masks we wear to convince one another that we are good Christians *etc.* who embody the values we proclaim when we tell one another how much we love our families *etc*.[31] Reinforced by such beliefs it is a relatively easy task to convince ourselves that there is no psyche apart from our conscious intentions, which have the added benefit of reflecting our best view of ourselves and our success in clothing ourselves in the ideological signs that reinforce this self-conception. And so when we give an account of our motives we simultaneously defend ourselves from charges that must remain obscure.

Traumatic events suggest that all of this may be no more than so many masks whereby we conceal from ourselves and others the motives that flourish whenever we act from the conflicts and desires that derive from everything unstable and hungry in us. In tragic inquiry the first thing eliminated is the defenses that hide the psyche from itself. They are supplanted by a willingness to cast off all beliefs and ideologies that protect us from confronting the dark places in the human heart. The key to probable reasoning in this Court is given only to those able to sustain (as Thomas and Smit cannot) the kind of psychological awareness that has always encountered strenuous resistance. A single canon of inquiry maintains here: one can never short-circuit the traumatic dimensions of the subject and the connections that define its scope. That is why the story of JonBenét Ramsey is as much a story of the crimes done to her before her death as it is a story of her murder. As much a story about her sexualization for the beauty pageants as it is about the sexual violation preceding and accompanying her death. It is why one can't stop with Patsy's action but must also discover John's and the complicity of both agents in an event that becomes more traumatic with each step of the investigation. It is also why there is no way to separate this story from an understanding of the social and sexual conflicts that are central to the American family in the dreams that vex and define it. In telling the story of the Ramseys one confronts of necessity a national epidemic—the sexual abuse of children—that cuts across class lines and that reflects a larger collective disorder: the belief of parents that they have a right to use their children to fulfill their unmet needs and desires and the even more insidious belief that doing so doesn't do lasting psychological damage to those children. And so to tell this story one must overcome everything in us that does not want it told. For the story of what happened to JonBenét Ramsey is also a story about us—about our voyeuristic interest in one kind of representation followed by our readiness to wash our hands of her lest we be forced to confront "thoughts beyond the reaches of our souls."

The kind of reasoning that informs this Court relieves us of one kind of concern—sheer empirical possibility—only to deepen the demands of another. That task is to take up the horror of what emerges as the most probable account consistent with the central data *and understand it from within*. Aristotle saw that tragedy focuses on the family because tragic events are most terrible when they happen in a situation that should be ruled by love and its responsibilities. In the Ramsey case understanding that horror turns on an understanding of sexuality as central to the human psyche. Freud is thus the tragic thinker of greatest value to the telling of this story, for what remains provocative, dangerous and valid in his thought is his willingness to see sexual conflict as the central drama of the family.

In confronting the resistance to confront what happened to JonBenét Ramsey one discovers the true burden of what it means to think psychologically. To think along such lines is to open oneself to painful feelings that only increase as the inquiry deepens and with no promise of catharsis and resolution to cushion the anguish such feelings open in the psyche. Thinking here involves a revolution in our emotional life—a reversal as abrupt and comprehensive as the one that occurs in Plato's Cave when the prisoners turn and confront the sunlight.

Our emotional life is, for the most part, a process of discharge, defense, and the reinforcing of self-esteem.[32] The function of what I term *the secondary emotions*—emotions such as contentment, pride, fear, and pity—is to provide the ego with ways to resolve conflict in a way that distances and protects it from the threat of disruptive experiences. Fear, for example, enables us to externalize anxiety by displacing inner conflicts into concern with matters external to the psyche. Pity short-circuits anxiety by turning suffering into something one experiences passively as undeserved misfortune. Contentment, as capstone, banishes the very sources of anxiety through the compulsive iteration of the sentiments that tranquilize the subject's relationship to itself.

There is, however, another order of emotions with a radically different office. The function of what I term *primary emotions*— emotions such as anxiety, humiliation, compassion, envy, and awe—

is to burden the *psyche* with an *agon* in which it finds its being existentially at issue and at risk.[33] Such emotions shatter the ego and activate the struggle of the psyche with itself, the struggle to confront its conflicts by eradicating everything in oneself that prevents such engagement. Anxiety, for example, is a suffered awareness of the control that the Other (parents, social and ideological forces, religious authorities) has in one's psyche experienced as the duty to reverse that control. Love is the refusal to succumb to the appeals of pity and the fixations of desire so that one may endeavor to conduct one's relationship to the beloved on the basis of uncompromising psychological honesty. Envy is the need to destroy anything that makes one feel contempt for oneself.

Primary emotion is a harsh taskmaster and for the most part human beings strenuously avoid it. But it comes to all of us now and then. It is what you felt perhaps the first time you saw a video of JonBenét and why you want to displace the anxiety of that image by shifting to the whodunit and the realm of purely factual questions. For to sustain that image is to deepen the pain of everything one comes to know about the case. Her image becomes the call to experience the traumatic not as something one relieves or resolves but as that which has not been constituted—and must be. Tragic psychological inquiry is one with the emotional challenge it poses, the challenge to abide within the realm of primary emotions and the agon they entail. To think in this way is to feel in ways that go against the grain of every attempt to shield ourselves from painful realities. Secondary emotions are an intrusion in this realm. Whenever they become needs superimposed upon the subject they violate the primary condition of tragic knowing. The think tragically is to experience the need to uproot everything in oneself that opposes the dynamic of primary emotions. Primary emotion is our access to the realm of tragic deeds, to what breeds about the hearts of the agents who perform them and what happens in the souls of those who suffer them. Secondary emotions, in contrast, always lead one away from the phenomena in keeping with their effort to tone down and soften what we thereby assure ourselves we will never understand.

For the tragic narrator what one can know is a function of what one can suffer. For suffering here is not the pang one seeks to relieve or discharge; it is the door of perception one tries to keep open so that one can deepen an awareness that comes only when sufferance is sustained. Suffering, for the tragic thinker, is not the "bitter duration" Rilke contemns, in which one waits passively for the cessation of what one cannot endure or comprehend. It is the opportunity to constitute a knowledge that is attained only when suffering begets the clarity of crystalline cognition.

We can now summarize the basic principles that shape what happens in this Court. To deliberate here one must: (1) sustain an in depth inquiry into the dark places of the psyche in opposition to all psychological needs and theories that oppose that effort; (2) sustain primary emotions and their development in opposition to the pull of secondary emotions and the Lethe they breed; (3) sustain the sufferance of one's subject by remaining true to what that subject does to you and then to make good that suffering by finding in it the ethic that informs one's writing.

Such is the true relationship between trauma and art. To write responsibly about traumatic events one cannot limit the claims of the trauma by imposing on it the needs and beliefs one had before one began to write. Writing is here inaugural and uniquely dangerous because it progressively challenges the entire structure of *guarantees* that inform the Western *ratio*.[34] They stand forth here as a concerted effort to deny the tragic by forcing it to yield meanings that deny everything it reveals as primary. Understanding is here the attempt to experience what the ratio cannot by *feeling* in a way that goes beyond the a priori limits that it imposes on experience. The psyche of the artist is at issue and at risk in tragic art because the process of discovery requires a self-overcoming in which one progressively deracinates everything in one's psyche that stands between oneself and the internalization of trauma. That internalization is the act from which understanding flows. The only legitimate way to respond to trauma is traumatically.[35] It is also, as I'll now argue, the basis for the only ethically authentic relationship to the audience.

19.

The common belief, of course, is that the duty of art is to respect and serve the needs of the audience. That belief takes many forms depending on the particular audience being served. There is the assumption, now dogma in an increasingly infantilized America, that art should never make us feel unpleasant things or if it does due care must be taken to coat them in reassurance, resolution, and recovery. What, after all, is the purpose of "entertainment" if not to relieve our cares and woes by reaffirming the feelings and beliefs that make life worth living. What we need—especially when faced with traumatic events (and on this think, for example, of what has happened in the arts since 9-11)[36]—is hope, deliverance, and the defense of those "positive" feelings we need lest pessimism seize a soul that finds it can't go on. An affective super-ego polices art. The mass audience, thoroughly indoctrinated in its ideology, stands firm in the belief that anything that makes us feel bad is bad. The duty of art—and now the argument ratchets itself up to the higher reaches of humanistic thought—is to uplift our hearts and strengthen our spirits by forming a *contract* with the reader promising that the reader's identity (read psyche) will never by threatened or traumatized by the artistic experience. Care must always be taken in representation to move *from* and *to* an affirmation of all the central humanistic guarantees.[37] That is so—and now the issue becomes one of artistic form—because unless a work is structured in such a way that it produces *catharsis* it is not a good work—aesthetically or morally. One may begin with disruptive emotions but everything must proceed toward their containment and discharge. An audience has a right to be assured that it will never be left with painful or unresolved feelings. Structure in art is the movement toward restoration and an affirmation of humanistic guarantees made stronger by their conquest of yet another unsettling phenomenon. Their power to impose themselves upon experience is, after all, what art is all about. The subtlest realization of these assumptions—and the most revealing in terms of the counter position I'm developing—is the program of Messianic or redemptive aesthetics. A quick example: Spielberg's *Schindler's List.* On which consider Stanley Kubrick's comment : "the holocaust is not about 6,000 Jews who were saved; it is about 6 million who weren't." Another example: Kushner's *Angels in America.* A redemptive aesthetic begins, of necessity, with the traumatic. No other subject is worth writing about. But while bathing itself in a direct depiction of horrifying phenomena, the movement of representation is toward finding what can be salvaged, retrieved for affirmative culture. Much, one finds, has been lost, the strength of such works beings their willingness to dispense with many ideological pieties, but the essential, humanistic contract remains in control. The teller of such tales is like Marlow before the beloved at the end of *Heart of Darkness.* Art must find that which redeems us from what would otherwise prove "too dark altogether." The traumatic cannot be "seen from itself," as Heidegger would put it, but can only be viewed by eyes intent on finding, then celebrating, every glimmer of hope and reassurance that can be wrested from the phenomena. And so once again the needs of the audience becomes the court to which everything is referred for a judgment that views the traumatic as valuable only if it can provide an opportunity for the restoration and celebration of the guarantees.[38]

The range of positions surveyed in the above paragraph chart the structure of ideological supplements that unite the average reader and the highly sophisticated one in a common goal—the containment of the traumatic through its subjection to demands antithetical to what one knows and feels when one engages trauma directly and from within. What we have in the positions surveyed above is the impossibility of serving two masters; of writing with one's subject in one hand and one's duty to the audience in the other in an unequal relationship in which the former is always sacrificed to the latter because the latter provides the *a priori* framework into which the former must be processed if it is to be intelligible, worthwhile, emotionally bearable.

There's only one thing awry here, but it derives from the central contradiction. Before a trauma can be resolved or "healed" it must be constituted. That is the artist's task—to internalize the traumatic and work from there without imposing *a priori* needs and guarantees upon it. Such an effort does not, I hasten to add, mean unrelieved horror or inevitable pessimism, as the servants of the guarantees are always quick to assert. They thereby miss the obvious. We don't know what it means because the effort has been proscribed. We don't know what can be found in tragic apprehension because "Don't go there"—Patsy Ramsey's command to investigators whenever they raised questions connected with the sexual—has been the dominant response of western culture to the tragic, however cleverly disguised. We have no way of assessing Nietzsche's idea that the tragic is one of "the highest forms of affirmation possible for an existing being" because we refuse to confront the tragic without the protection provided by the guarantees. As a result, however, we are unable to preserve the claims of the only audience that matters.

20.

For in writing about the Ramsey case there is only one audience that matters. That audience is composed of a single member: JonBenét Ramsey. "The dead remain in danger," as Walter Benjamin taught. The primary danger is their sacrifice to the emotional needs of the audience. That is why the Court of tragic art entails the working of a unique form of Justice, which is also the only justice JonBenét can now hope to receive. It is that justice which abjures catharsis and all the ways we sacrifice the claims of the dead the moment they threaten our emotional needs. A tragic work of art is like Hamlet's Mousetrap. The task of tragic representation is to expose our resistance to the tragic by constructing representations that lead the audience to feel what an authentic experience of the subject demands. An ethic of tragic representation is defined by this act; the cathartic, redemptive, audience friendly view of art is its inadvertent parody. Tragic representation systematically undercuts all the ideas, beliefs, values, and emotions that we impose on tragic subjects in order to protect ourselves from them. The danger to the dead is thereby negated in the only way it can be, through an assault on everything in us that conspires to deny their experience. In contrast to narratives shaped by principles that assure emotional relief, the Court of tragic art is dedicated to acts of authentic mourning which endeavor to internalize what happened to the dead in order to speak not about but from their experience.

21.

Which is why the true danger to this Court is internal. I refer to the predictable production and enthusiastic reception of works that are seen as definitive because they take up issues of deep concern to a large public (thus fulfilling the mandate given by the legal system) and treat them in a way that protects and delivers the audience from them. Troubling events haunt those members of a society who have not managed to block or extinguish awareness, those, for example, who remember JonBenét and all that has since been in the news about the murder and sexual violation of young women. A diverse audience seeks in the psychological probability that literature affords a way to wrestle with such issues and find, if possible, a collective understanding. And thus a place was prepared long before its appearance for Alice Sebold's *The Lovely Bones*, a work hailed by high-brow critics and a large, popular audience as a work of enduring value in enabling us in effect to work through the trauma of JonBenét Ramsey and the growing list of young girls subjected to similar fates.[39]

22.

To set the stage for the theoretical point I want to make about this book I'll draw two things from Daniel Mendelsohn insightful critique of the work in *The New York Review of Books*.[40] First, these key facts about the work's reception and Sebold's lightning rise to literary prominence: (1) May 22, 2003 (6 weeks before its official publication date) *New York Times* columnist Anna Quindlen hawks the book on the *Today* show as an essential work destined to be a classic; (2) within days it becomes number 1 on Amazon.com; (3)

within 4 months it is in its 18th printing, with over 2 million copies in print; (4) a chorus of reviews appear praising the work for what Michael Pietsch (its publisher) terms "its fearless and ultimately redemptive portrayal of 'dark material;'" (5) these sentiments are echoed, Mendelsohn notes, by "the remarkably high number of customer reviews (over 800) that have thusfar appeared on amazon.com. Second, as Mendelsohn's article makes clear, what we have here is not a literary event but an ideological one: the need of the media, the culture industry, and the general public to hail Sebold's ability to confront the "dark material" that has been preying on our national consciousness and wrestle it, Proteus-like, to a richly nuanced and deeply human understanding. That is the claim made on behalf of the book and, as Mendelsohn shows, nothing could be further from the truth. "Darkness, grief, and heartbreak is what *The Lovely Bones* scrupulously avoids. This is the real heart of its appeal." Its scenes, as in a TV movie of the week, have the "predictable arcs of crisis, healing, and closure." Everything is "in soft focus," especially "the novel's sketchy attempts to confront the face of evil." The vaunted lyricism of the work is "nonsense that has the superficial prettiness you associate with the better class of greeting cards." What Sebold offers is "feel-good redemption, ""healing with no real mourning." For, as Mendelsohn concludes, "the real point of Sebold's novel isn't to make you confront dreadful things, but, if anything, to assure you that they have no really permanent consequences." What the book signals is not an achievement but a crisis—the desperate need to promote the application of the Hallmark sensibility to a traumatic issue so that we can assure ourselves that the two principles of successful therapy, insight and working through (*Durcharbeit*), have been honored in what has really been no more than an occasion to congratulate ourselves by indulging a bevy of good feelings. The lionization of this book is the nadir of "affirmative" culture.

What makes all this particularly significant is the claim that the book of necessity makes for itself. Sebold's novel, you see, is narrated by the dead girl. Sebold will boldly go where tragic representation must—into the consciousness of the victim and represent her voice from within. Everyone has a dim awareness that this is the point of view that has not been honored and that has a singular claim on our attention. A trauma filtered through some voice outside the trauma—whether omniscient or limited—will always remain suspect. What is needed is the voice of the violated, a voice speaking from the depths of traumatized experience. Sebold will go where Thomas and Smit cannot, into a consciousness that only an artist can fathom because the genius of poetic language, as Aristotle notes, is to find the metaphors and images required to *plot* the progression of the violated psyche in the dark passage of its attempt to fathom what was done to it. Everything rests on Sebold's ability to enter that consciousness and find words adequate to a violation that is never finished and that remains everpresent at the center of consciousness. The horror of sexual abuse is that it never ends. For it creates a psyche defined by a burden that is never lifted, an anguish that informs every intimate experience, a door of perception that never closes. Violation creates the conflicts of a psyche that bears its violation as the center of every experience.

Susie, the narrator of Sebold's novel, is the antithesis of such a consciousness. Sebold assures she will be so by muting the scene of her violation and by transporting Susie from the beginning of her tale to "heaven." With her ascension to that realm Susie achieves that acquiescence in her fate that gives her the ability to dispense love, compassion, sympathy and understanding on those she looks down upon from a perspective freed of their wants and cares. Susie stands at a wistful distance from her own experience, from what she suffered and all she has lost. What we have in here, in effect, is another instance of the comforting myth that children can't understand or internalize what happens to them. Susie's body is violated but her psyche remains clean, almost pristine. Transcendence has never been better. Susie has no regrets save one. Believe it or not, toward the end of the book she is transported into the body of a friend so that she can experience the first joy of sexual love, this the books furthest reach in its effort to represent the consciousness of its beloved. The allusion to Toni Morrison in the previous sentence is deliberate. The appropriate comparison. Morrrison's effort in *Beloved* is to sustain and constitute the traumatic by representing a consciousness that is defined—utterly—by it. She then sets that psyche loose to work upon the psyches of the survivors so that they are brought back into the space of the traumatic as that awareness that forever deepens and never ends. It is the legacy that the dead bequeath as sufferance to the living. As Morrison's narrator notes, "This is not a story to pass on." Sebold's, on the other hand, is because it is one with Lou Smits' effort to dispense the balm of an unshakeable Christian world view and one with Steve Thomas's to deflect attention from the sexual so that it becomes no more than an evanescent and peripheral phenomenon.

Susie is not the traumatic subject. She's the perfect corpse at the perfect funeral—a funeral held for the benefit of the living with the dead whispering to us everything we need to hear so that we can rest assured that she understands, forgives, and loves us and is at peace with herself in a cleansed awareness. Nothing traumatic intrudes on such a consciousness because such consciousness is attained not through a principled engagement of the traumatic but by its systematic avoidance. Susie is a saint and Sebold makes her that way in order to protect the audience from reality.

23.

I here offer a summary of the principles that inform the proceedings of a Court devoted to Tragic Justice. This section thereby makes explicit the central concepts implicit in the preceding discussions.

I. Probable reasoning about traumatic events is the reconstruction from a body of facts of the psychological motives that drive agents when they act from the conflicts and desires central to the psyche. Such reasoning is based on the attempt to make primary emotion the principle of cognition enabling one to probe and sustain the full dimensions of a traumatic subject.

II. The Traumatic is any event or image that tears open the psyche, exposing it to the claims of everything that the ego and affirmative culture strives to deny. A crisis happens in the soul. One faces the fundamental choice: one can either sustain the burden of existential consciousness or give oneself over to the process of inner deadening.

The traumatic dimensions of experience are for the most part repressed. That repression is the origin and office of the ego. Psyche, in contrast, is the relationship one lives to the wounds and conflicts that define one's being. Traumatic events restore our contact with that register. Those who sustain the resulting anxiety enter on the long path that leads to tragic knowledge. For trauma does two things to the psyche: (1) it delivers it over to catastrophic anxiety; i.e., to the threat of psychic dissolution in unspeakable pain and nameless dread; and (2) it attunes it to the *cruelty* at the heart of human relations. Knowledge for such a subject becomes the attempt to understand that cruelty in depth by rejecting the appeal of all thoughts, beliefs, and feelings that would ameliorate that cruelty or shield us from it. Internalizing the traumatic is the act that gives birth to the tragic sensibility, the act that is the origin of tragic knowing. Tragic reasoning is probable reasoning from inside the darkest and most deeply repressed places in the human heart. Its office is to know what we don't want to know about ourselves.

III. Literature is that public forum devoted to a psychological and emotional knowledge of what other public forums are unable to comprehend. Their limits are its starting point. Its task is to constitute the psychological knowledge that other discourses proscribe, severely limit, or imprison in insoluble conceptual *aporias*. While other public forums exist to celebrate and transmit the ideological beliefs that protect us from ourselves, the function of art is to provide a forum dedicated to the public airing of secrets, the public representation of the conflicts and contradictions central to our culture. This forum is defined by a unique relationship to the audience. The purpose of serious literature is to make an audience feel, in primary ways, what it doesn't want to feel and to refuse to release the audience from those feelings. That is why psychological inquiry here is also incipient political action. Serious literature attempts to perform a revolution in the psyche— one that will lead to a complete transformation of how one relates to one's world.

IV. Tragic art is the fullest realization of these imperatives. The tragic is the attempt to understand the psychological causes that give birth to horrifying deeds in the realm of human relations. The purpose of such art is not to resolve traumatic experiences but to constitute them. It is that way of knowing that preserves the claims of the traumatic against all our attempts to flee, repress, or deny it.

The tragic thinker attempts to understand human beings in terms of the primary emotions that drive them by suffering those emotions within oneself. That act is what generates knowledge in this realm. In humanistic terms, tragic thinking is the attempt to internalize the "human meaning" of what happens when we do tragic things. The effort of the tragic thinker is to get at the primary emotions from which people act and suffer; to feel those emotions at an equally primary register; and to use that knowledge as the basis for reconstructing their tale in a way that will preserve its tragic character. Sustaining tragic awareness requires the ability to live within the realm of primary emotions. Such emotions are the source of our deepest self-knowledge because they create and exacerbate an anxiety in which we are at issue and at risk with no inner distance between *who* we are and what we feel. To *be* is here to *take action within oneself* with no defenses or delays possible, no way to shuffle off the burden that such emotions impose on us. The tragic is thus a fundamental challenge to anyone who pursues it. For it places one demand on us: fundamental change.

The duty of the tragic thinker is not to discharge or "cathart" the burden of such knowledge, but to draw out its implications by constructing narratives that will establish the connections that tragic understanding reveals as central to human experience. A tragic tale is about the connections that entangle human beings in a destructive web of interrelated conflicts. That is the real meaning of *plot*, which Aristotle correctly termed "the soul of tragedy." A tragic tale is about the terrible unity that binds human beings to one another in the inexorable progression of and toward terrible events. Plot traces the progression of a system of connected conflicts as they affect the one (or ones) who suffers them most deeply. In some cases this is the experience of an old man, as in *King Lear*; in others the acute awareness of a mind ahead of its time and thus condemned to know what others deny, as in *Hamlet*; in O'Neill's great play it is the collective awareness toward which an entire family moves; and sometimes it is the experience of a child who suffers because she has no way to distance herself from those around her and who sacrifices herself, as only a child can, in the desperate effort to heal her parents. A tragic plot is the fathoming of a complex set of interrelationships in terms of the central conflict that informs them in its movement toward catastrophe.

Aristotle was doubly wrong in seeing secondary emotions (pity and fear) and their catharsis as the purpose of tragic literature. The task of the tragic thinker is to sustain the traumatic force of primary emotions. Most theories of tragedy can most profitably be understood as attempts to contain and deny the tragic: to impose upon it conceptual (the flaw) or emotional (catharsis) guarantees in order to limit its significance and thereby deliver us from the primary emotions that tragic experience opens up in us. The tragic is a challenge to all other ways of knowing, all other ways of being. Rather than one way of viewing the world among others, the tragic exposes the truth of ideology: i.e., that all ideologies have as their common function the attempt to establish beliefs and commonplaces that will give a group the certitudes it needs to protect it from what it doesn't want to know about itself. In psychoanalytic terms, the tragic is the condensation of human awareness; everything else is its displacement. The tragic sensibility is opposed to all efforts to "manage" trauma by adapting it to the defensive needs of the ego. Psychologically, the task is to deracinate everything in the psyche that shields us from self-knowledge. Politically, the task is to expose all the fine sentiments and conceptual guarantees that we impose upon traumatic events in order to domesticate them.[41]

To conclude, tragic thinking is probable reasoning about the psyche that sustains the traumatic and unlocks its cognitive power. What that act teaches us is that our problem is not that we can't know what most likely happened in the Ramsey case. Our problem is that we can't sustain the emotions that such knowledge entails.[42] It is our courage, not our ability to make inferences, that is at fault. We fail because we refuse to know ourselves; to know the dark places in the human heart and sustain that knowledge against the desire to flee and deny it. The concern of the tragic writer is never simply with a whodunit or a docudrama. As in Faulkner's *Absalom, Absalom!,* the "facts" are only a beginning. The task is to create the psyche of the actors and thereby preserve the horror of their deeds. In pursuing that task tragic thinking is beyond Keats'"negative capability." It is the ability to exist in catastrophic anxiety and make that condition the door of perception. One thereby sustains the recognition that in the realm of human relations the avidities of the psyche exceed all other principles. They are prior to and create the possibility of love, which is the effort to overcome the primary condition that binds us to one another.

V. The previous section indicates why the family is the primary subject of tragedy. Parenting is the transmission of one's psychological conflicts and one's unmet and unconscious desires to one's children. This is the act that founds the family. A family is the conflicts between the parents as they form the psyches of the children. Psyche is the attempt to mediate the conflicts that our parents invested in us. Psychological birth is not some natural maturation process made possible by the ability of our parents to bracket their psyches while they transmit the "bonds of love" which produce a stable, impermeable identity.[43] We are who we are as the product of our parent's conscious and unconscious conflicts. Aristotle was only half right. Tragedy focuses on the family because tragedy is about the freight that love bears—the deep and desperate needs it tries to fulfill at the expense of those it is projected upon.

There is no escaping any of this for the simplest of reasons. What we don't know or won't face about ourselves is what we do—to the other. This is never more true than in our most intimate relationships. That is why love, in most cases, quickly becomes the contract to deny or protect one another from that which each psyche refuses to acknowledge. Which thereby festers in conflicts that must come a cropper. The primary lesson failed relationships teach those who learn from them is that the end was in the beginning—in the conflicts both agents refused to confront and the pattern of relating that derived from that refusal. This is so because intimacy is not the place where our conflicts are magically dissolved but where they are necessarily engaged. To be intimate is to experience the anxiety of opening oneself to another. It is, of necessity, an experience in which one's deepest conflicts rise to the surface. They are then confronted or in most cases projected and denied. That is, lodged in the other as the burden of what they cannot know or must bear in silence. Love is in most cases the process in which couples adapt themselves to one another's defenses in order to avoid what the other teaches them must remain repressed. Intimacy, which could be the process of coming to know everything one doesn't want to know about oneself, thus becomes a mutual cover-up dedicated to the perpetual deferral of the conflicts that thereby become the cancer at the center of the relationship. Its development accordingly becomes the action (or plot) through which these conflicts mature to the point of crisis: the point at which one or both agents discovers that there is nothing left in the relationship and so one must acquiesce in inner death or take some action to break out of one's prison. As Freud showed—and this is his central unacknowledged message—the reality of the "unconscious," the repressed, is that it is active. Never moreso, as the above considerations imply, than in our parenting.

For the sad fact is that in most cases a child doesn't complete a love; it is an attempt to make up for what is lacking in it. It gives the parents a way to seek out what they can't find in each other or to act out all that remains avid in themselves. To be a child is to be assigned a role in an unfolding drama that is defined by the conflicts of and between the parents. Some parents, like Patsy Ramsey, invest their conflicts and desires in overt and hysterical ways; others do so subtly but just as pervasively. For there is no way one relates that doesn't bear the brunt of one's character. Say what he will, a loveless and withdrawn man will, as father, transmit that coldness to his child as the deep doubt the child internalizes about whether it is capable or worthy of love. A sexually repressed parent transmits that condition to their child, creating the conflicts that will define that child's relationship to its sexuality. What the parent needs, fears, desires, denies—this is what the child perceives as what it is called on to mediate. A child's psyche is the attempt to know the psyche of its parents in a way that is more fundamental than any other form of knowledge—to know it feelingly. In the child intimacy reveals its other face, the one couples learn to conceal and deny. For in intimacy one gives oneself away: one reveals one's conflicts in the act of investing them in those who will bear them as their burden. The act that defines childhood is the attempt to know the psyche of one's parents by fathoming what is expressed in the ways they relate to us when they are most intimate with us or most rejecting of the intimacy we try to form with them. The family is the place of the greatest suffering, the greatest wounds, because it is the place where in intimacy the parents reveal the truth about themselves to those who internalize that knowledge as their psychological birth, those who experience it traumatically as the seed-bed of conflicts from which they can find no escape.

In the family the wheel comes full circle. What one hasn't worked through in oneself is necessarily passed on to one's children as their burden. As in the *Oresteia*, one deed begets another often more extreme or deadly in a process in which everyone gets progressively more deeply entangled in the nets that bind them. (In this regard, an important unwritten chapter in JonBenét's story concerns Patsy's mother, Nedra, the original author of the beauty queen obsession and an eager proponent of the need for Patsy to procure help in teaching JonBenét how to "sex up" her performance.) The central truth about the family is this: when parents project their conflicts rather than confronting them they pass them on in a way that begets deeper conflicts with no end to the process save senseless suffering or tragic action by one who dares to know what the family refuses to know about itself. A tragic understanding of the family is a stern taskmaster. It foregrounds what our piety denies: that the more loudly a family proclaims its happiness and its realization of cultural ideals the more the conflicts it suppresses fester as the general atmosphere everyone breathes, especially those who sense the underlying pressure and the tragic task laid on them, to sacrifice themselves in order to keep the dance going. There is, of course, one antidote to this, an impossible one. Before one becomes a parent one should overcome one's conscious and unconscious conflicts. That is the only way to guarantee that one won't pass it on. But for that to happen brutal honesty would have to be the contract that unites the loving couple—from the beginning.

VI. The above is the necessary prelude to understanding the drama in which it all becomes concrete—sexuality.

Sexuality is the central experience in which the conflicts of the family coalesce. That is so because in its origin the sexual is the experience in which the child's openness to the parents in love is met by the parent's need to invest their desires and conflicts in the child. Parents project their sexual conflicts by sexualizing the child in the way demanded by their psyche. Sometimes by making the child become a beauty queen. Or an altar boy and future priest. Or a jock, shamed in defeat, gloating in victory. A withdrawn obsessional incapable of emotional intimacy. A narcissist unfeeling in the use of others for a single pleasure—the polishing of one's souless self-image. Sexuality is the key to any family because it is where the conflicts of and between the parents are acted out in a way that must perforce be internalized by the child. For most couples intimacy may be the contract not to confront certain things. Such luxury is denied the child. Intimacy for the child is the necessity to internalize what the parents make one feel because *for a child what one feels is who one is*. There's no inner distance separating the subject from itself; no defenses yet; no way to be anything other than who one becomes as a result of what one feels. Feeling is here the origin of the conflicts one lives as those conflicts are born in the way one experiences one's *body-psyche*. Psychosexual identity is the drama in which one's own desire and its conflicts are formed as precipitates of what one *feels* in one's body in those experiences in which one is *closest* to one's parents; i.e., *those experiences in which their desires and conflicts are experienced by us as our own*. We are as incarnate consciousness (body-psyche) the product of the experiences in which we offered ourselves in an attempt to comprehend and satisfy what we perceived as the desperate needs and wishes of our parents. A child's psyche is the harsh truth and *agon* of love experienced in its origin—the taking of another into oneself in the attempt to *be* what that other requires. Of all formations sexuality is the deepest because it creates a body-psyche that is inseparable from the conflicts one must struggle to mediate whenever intimacy reawakens the claims and violations of one's earliest loves.[44] One then experiences that which is deeper in us than anything else—the wound that we are. In abusing a child, psychologically and/or physically, one does permanent damage because one creates a psyche bound to the wound that defines it. In sexuality one experiences the truth of one's psyche and conveys that truth to the other no matter how cleverly one may try to disguise the signs. Psychosexual identity is the core of the psyche. We are who we are as a result of the kind of intimacy we experienced in our earliest relationships. That is why sexual experience is the living out of the conflicts that define us. It is the test of our ability to achieve intimacy by overcoming the conflicts that are the legacy of our founding intimacies or the place where we suffer the consequences of that failure.

In founding that drama the family is once again the place where the wheel comes full circle. The family is the end result of what their parents did to our parents as that legacy is transmitted to us as the beginning of what we in turn do to our children. It is in the family that the psyche is formed and to the family that it returns either to propagate its conflicts or, finally, to confront them. There is no way to avoid this drama. It is the act that makes us human. And as such it as the drama from which other dramas derive. For what happens in the family forms the basis of what happens whenever we love, experience sexual intimacy, and as parents pass on to our children the results of what happened to us when we struggled to deal with what was invested in us when we were very young.

These reflections enable us to formulate what would have been easily misunderstood before.

Incestual conflict is the reality that unites and defines the family. It is how the unmet and unconscious conflicts in the sexual relationship between the parents informs the relationship that each parent forms to the child: the compensation sought, the revenge planned, the substitute found with whom one can have the intimacy that one's partner denies or that one denies one's partner. So understood, the incestual is a category far broader than the overtly sexual. In fact, its most insidious form lies in what may be termed *emotional incest*. This occurs whenever one or both parents give a child the message that they are dependent on the child for their emotional or psychological well-being; that the child fulfills for them needs the mate cannot fulfill. Equally destructive in such cases is the relationship that the spurned mate forms to a child who has been turned into an oedipal rival. In such a tangled web all conflicts meet and become progressively more intense in the one who of necessity internalizes and must perforce try to mediate them. "Who shows a child as they are" must reveal the formation of psychosexual identity as the experience in which the sexual conflicts of and between one's parents take root in the child in a way that defines the child's psyche, delivering it over to the inherently tragic effort to mediate those conflicts one internalized as offers that can't be refused. That is why deracination is the only authentic relationship one can live to who one is.

The line of thought about psyche, sexuality, and the family that I've outlined here, and developed at length elsewhere,[45] constitutes the most deeply resisted contribution of psychoanalysis to our self-understanding. It also reveals where the real resistance to psychoanalysis lies. Psychoanalysis (like Shakespearean tragedy) calls our attention to what is in front of us; to what can be known and even achieve the status of common sense if we look at our lives with honesty rather than mendacity. That's why it's so convenient to fixate on the question of whether or not "it's a science" and so comforting to be informed by the latest scientific knowledge, as formulated by cognitive biologist Steven Pinker, that incest is a rare almost nonexistent occurrence among humans because evolution has wired us in a way that renders it undesirable.[46]

The question whether psychoanalysis is a science is finally a bogus one. For psychoanalysis is an art—and an inherently tragic one. Freud noted, "one can find in my thought the basis for a very grave philosophy." This is not, of course, the way his thought has been appropriated by the bulk of his followers, especially in America, where everything dangerous and disruptive in psychoanalysis succumbs to the demand for adaptation, normalcy, and the protection of the defense-ego, that part of the psyche that is, as Winnicott put it, vigorously opposed to reality; i.e., to an understanding of the unconscious conflicts we project in all the affairs of our daily life and their roots in the psychosexual conflicts that define the only identity we have. Psychoanalysis is a call to bear the duties of tragic awareness. Freud finally protected himself from the full force of that knowledge. Our task is to constitute it.[47]

CASTING THE AUDIENCE: TOWARD A THEATRE OF PRIMARY EMOTIONS

1.

The commercial theatre needs no manifesto. It gets its from season-ticket sales: Do nothing that will make the evening's entertainment harder to digest than the fine meal the audience consumed an hour before as prelude to the after-dinner sleep in which they dream their way toward final curtain. Everything passes through the cuisinart of an overriding need: to create those feelings that relieve and resolve whatever is troubling. "That's entertainment." This motive, which has always been the bane of our theatre, became in the wake of 9-11 a national imperative. A traumatized nation called out for healing and the arts responded with a virtually single-minded effort to produce works distinguished by nothing other than the attempt to bathe the collective psyche in the Lethe of happy talk, heroic posturing, sentimentalism, and nostalgia. Affirmative culture today apes the spirit of Lynne Cheney's NEA in giving us a theatre at home in its *polis*, one that caters to its emotional needs. Such a theatre knows what it is and why it is; and, more importantly, what kinds of plays and productions must be cancelled as "inappropriate at this time." Our problem is that we've lost the ability to distinguish ourselves from this theatre. We've lost it because we've lost an understanding of our foundations, an understanding of what the purpose of theatre has been since its origin.

2.

From its inception theatre has had a unique cultural function. It is the one public forum where people come together to witness the exposure of things that they don't want to know—about themselves. Other public forums exist to celebrate the ideological beliefs that protect us from ourselves. The public sphere is, by and large, the space of ideological *interpellation*; i.e., the hailing operations that tell us what we believe and feel as subjects subjected by the social order to share articles of faith and meaning which have as their primary function the blinding of subjects to their historical situation. The purpose of public forums—the Sunday sermon, the media, presidential addresses—is to offer rituals of pseudo-deliberation that always move to the triumphant reassertion of the unchanging truths that constitute the collective affirmation of who we are and what we value. We come together as an audience in public space to participate in a group psychology in which conflict is overcome and calm of mind restored. Public space, in late capitalism, is the arena in which we are put collectively to sleep.

Authentic theatre is the exception. A primary constituent of the magic that attends it is the will of an audience to sit in rapt attention before the public airing of secrets that expose them to themselves. When a play does its work the audience finds itself, like Claudius, caught in a mousetrap as the characters on the stage reveal the hidden conflicts of the audience. Such is the true measure of our responsibility and of how deeply an audience can find itself delivered into our hands.

3.

The purpose of theatre is to move an audience from the comfort of secondary emotions to the agon of primary emotions.

Secondary emotions (pity, fear, contentment) constitute the defenses that the ego has developed to displace and discharge anxiety. The motives the ego requires for its maintenance—safety and self-esteem—find in secondary emotions the means to resolve conflict in a way that distances and protects the ego from the threat of all disruptive experiences. (I am, of course, aware that Aristotle taught us that pity and fear are the deep, tragic emotions. One may take the continued hegemony of that view as a sign of how far we are from the kind of theatre we must create.)

Pity—the effort to short-circuit anxiety by turning suffering into something one can only experience passively as undeserved misfortune that comes as a result of factors over which one has no control and limited responsibility

Fear—the effort to externalize anxiety by displacing inner conflict into concern with matters outside the psyche.

Contentment—the feeling of well-being that banishes all sources of anxiety through the obsessive-compulsive iteration of the sentiments that tranquilize the subject's relationship to itself.

Primary emotions (anxiety, humiliation, envy, cruelty, melancholia), in contrast, burden the subject with an agon in which it finds that its being existentially at issue and at risk. Such emotions are defined by the absence of any inner distance between what one feels and who one is. One is assaulted from within by the force of the conflicts that are central to one's being.

Anxiety—existence as the awareness of responsibility to reverse the control that the other (parents, social and ideological forces, religious authorities) has over one's psyche.

Envy—the need to destroy anything that makes one feel contempt for oneself or that activates the memory of possibilities one has squandered.

Melancholia—Keats' "wakeful anguish of the soul;" the desire to engage the core-conflicts of one's psyche in active reversal.

Compassion—love as the refusal to succumb to the appeals of pity and the fixations of desire so that one may conduct one's relationship to others on the basis of uncompromising psychological honesty.

Cruelty—the desire to poison what is vital in another's psyche so that one can watch the other bring about their own destruction.

Primary emotion shatters the ego and awakens the psyche. The **ego** is the system of defenses whereby an illusory identity is maintained through vigorous opposition to two things: reality and the inner world. **Psyche** is the agon that is joined whenever that system breaks down and the subject is forced to engage the conflicts of its inner world. Secondary emotion is the system of feelings we construct in order to deliver us from that process. The purpose of theatre is to activate the latter process.

4.

"The director's first task is to cast the audience." (Grotowski) Something I want from you is opposed to something you want from me. That is the essence of drama. It is also the relationship between any worthwhile play and the audience. The *theatre event* is what happens *between* an ensemble and the audience as the former work upon the latter to activate a group psychology of a unique kind. A written play is nothing but a score that is only actualized when in performance an audience begins to move as one to the urgencies of a collective psychology. We don't create in front of an audience; we create by working on an audience. They give us their defenses and we give them back to them as primary emotions.

That dynamic is the main difference between cinema and theatre. Cinema is oneiric: the projection of private fantasies by subjects sitting alone in the dark. Theatre is communal: lived and living because it is built in performance out of the responses that the ensemble seizes upon in order to take an audience in directions it fears to tread. At the movies audience members try to be unaware of one another; in theatre they desperately depend upon and solicit one another's responses in the effort to evolve a collective psychology. Theatre takes on its inherent danger when the ensemble uses this condition to activate an agon that shatters the ideological beliefs that hold the audience together. When we cast the audience in ways that flatter their self-esteem and reinforce their beliefs we create a theatre in which nothing happens. When in casting them we seek out the agons that will engage what is buried most deeply within them we create a theatre that shimmers with existential possibility. To bring that about our task is to overturn the wisdom of Stoppard's Player-King: "audiences know what to expect and that is all they can believe." Most productions, unfortunately, bank on that fact, drawing their mandate from the pleasure associated with repetition of habitual operations whereas for us the purpose of playing must be to make what happens on the stage become for the audience what the Archaic Torso of Apollo was for Rilke: "For here there is no place that does not see you/You must change your life." The paradigmatic status of O'Neill's *The Iceman Cometh* for an understanding of the theatre event derives from O'Neill's effort of that work to dramatize the essence of this process. Hickey engages the audience on stage in a process that represents the agon that any great play strives to activate in the theatre audience.

5.

The art of acting is defined by this agon. That art can be condensed into an aphorism: "something must break within you with each line." (Angelina Jolie) In exploring the inner world actors don't discover their "true self" and their "true feelings." They discover the inner conflicts that must be engaged in order to uncover what one does not want to know about oneself. When one acts from that place acting becomes, as Jack Nicholson said, "the process of dripping acid on the nerves." For when something breaks within you with each line it breaks too within the audience who see their world represented in a way that unmasks it. Robert DeNiro's great description of acting is only as good as its hidden major premise. To quote DeNiro: "Actors are like people. They don't express their emotions. They conceal them. And it is in the process of concealing them that the emotions are revealed." An audience experiences the shock of recognition when they are confronted with action and gestures that perfectly mimic their characteristic ways of fleeing themselves. The question marks that the Brechtian actor places within and at the end of each line are addressed, contra Brecht, not just to the intellect but to the psyche: they plant in the head the time-bomb that explodes in the heart as primary emotions erupt from long concealment engaging the audience in the struggle to confront and reverse their lives. The purpose of acting is not to entertain, but, borrowing from Albee's George, to "get the guests."

6.

Here is a story revealing where drama begins. Recently, by chance, I saw on television a dinner party held by Oprah Winfrey for six members of her Book Club and Toni Morrison. Among the guests where several obviously wealthy socialites (including one named Celeste). At the end of a bountiful dinner, Toni Morrison reads from the passage toward the end of *The Song of Solomon* in which Pilate mourns her dead grandchild Hagar. During the reading Celeste breaks down and weeps uncontrollably. Comforted by Morrison, that great-souled presence, who holds her, Celeste, still weeping, tells her story. Her first child was still-born. She never saw the child nor did she ask to hold it. "I was always taught that I should be protected from such things." But now something different has come into being, thanks to Morrison's work. "I never held my baby. I'm so ashamed." A drama has begun. A work of art has put a subject in touch with a depth in her psyche that she did not know existed. One can only imagine the struggle later that night to resume the mask and cover her embarrassment when Celeste returns to her suburban home and, one imagines, the wealthy friends gathered together to watch her on Oprah and celebrate the occasion. She can't go home again—and yet she must. Such is the power, however momentary, of art to cut through our defenses and "make us ashamed of our existence" (Sartre). As Celeste learned, art restores us to the past that matters by revealing that past as the forgotten duties that we bear to our own humanity. Through art they are imposed on us in the violence of the claim they make upon us. And so our anxiety for Celeste is that she will succeed, helped by her group to say what Heidegger says we always saw once anxiety passes: "it was nothing." Theatre is the attempt to bring that nothing into being.

7.

"An image is true insofar as it is violent." (Artaud) The task of the playwright is to find traumatic images and then create a dramatic structure that will unleash their power so that the emotional *dynamis* implicit in the image becomes an agon that transforms the audience's relationship to itself. Theatre must preserve the violence of the image because without that violence nothing happens. Change only becomes possible when an image stays alive and works within the psyche, when another's suffering becomes one's own and one gains no relief from that suffering through fine thoughts and airy platitudes. Our task is to create a theatre that knows, with the artist R. B. Kitaj that "reducing complexity is a ruse," that the goal of art is "to create images that will sit in the Unconscious" for it is there, where nothing sits still, that change begins in psyches delivered over to everything they hoped keep repressed. Such a theatre can be as grand as Weiss' *Marat/Sade* or as intimate as Chekhov's dream of that actor who reveals his fate (and ours) in the way he lifts his coffee-cup or turns the pages of his newspaper. The choice does not lie between an "epic" and an intimate theatre. It lies between exploring the truth of primary emotions or indulging the evasions of secondary emotions. The lesson Artaud taught visits our consciousness daily. It has become what Hegel called the newspaper: "the morning prayer of modern man." On rising one turns on the TV and is awash in traumatic images, as in a six year old child mimicking the dance and gestures of an adult woman in a "beauty pageant" soliciting our voyeuristic complicity in the illness that tells parents they have a right to do such things to children. And so we look again and see what gives the image its true violence. It's there—in the deadened eyes, and the broken, frightened gestures that rupture the performance from within, giving it a Brechtian function that is one with the ability of JonBenét Ramsey to "signal through the flames." In such images we recover the lesson we most need to recover: that drama is the truth of everyday life; because agon remains the being of the subject. In the image of a child violating herself in a desperate effort to win her parent's love we are offered a way back into Aristotle's recognition that tragedy has the family as its primary subject because cruelty is most terrible when we find it where we had expected to find love. For we then suffer the recognition that one sign of our disorder is the pleasure the culture took—and continues to take—from such images. In the traumatic image the suppressed truths of our world assault us in their inherent violence. To articulate their meaning requires a descent into the heart of our collective disorders.

8.

"Always historicize." (Frederic Jameson) Theatre in its origin is wedded to this principle. The contradictions of its time are its subject matter. That is why the task of theatre is always the same—and always different: to expose *ideology* by creating dramatic forms and dramatic experiences that cannot be subsumed under the guarantees that ideology superimposes on experience in order to assure us that traumatic realities and conflicts cannot alter or destroy what we desperately need to believe: that we possess an *identity* that is one with the goodness of a *human nature* that cannot be lost and that guarantees the persistence of values that are universal and a-historical. In combating ideology we face a redoubtable task. For these assumptions and guarantees are not the property of a single ideology. They go much deeper, forming a common heritage. Insofar as we are creatures of the *logos*, the western *ratio*, we structure experience in terms of a *system of guarantees*. They form the *a priori* frame of reasoning, explanation, and emotional response that we impose upon events so that nothing traumatic can impinge upon the ego-identity that the guarantees provide. The logos or ratio can be defined, for our purposes, as the system of intellectualizing operations that give experience a structure that is conceptually transparent and that marginalizes—as irrational, neurotic, unintelligible, irresponsible—anything that fails to correspond to reason. Such a system offers us an essentialized identity that frees us from contingency and that provides a way, especially in times of national crisis, to transcend particular political and factional differences and unite as subjects on the basis of a shared, universal humanity.

We discern here the true reason Plato banished the poets from the perfect state. The agons drama explores and the primary emotions it engages exceed the forms of mediation that the ratio provides. Drama offers knowledge of ways of being that are lived concretely by agents who act from principles of psychological and existential self-mediation that exceed reason and its founding desire—to submit experience to that which can be rationally conceptualized. Drama is our way of representing and apprehending all that exceeds that framework. In that effort reason is no more than the cutting edge of passion and oversteps its bounds whenever it presumes to legislate over that which it must humbly serve.

9.

Fortunately there is a concrete way to pursue this theme, a way that dialectically connects history and drama. History under the ratio is the explanations that are constructed to deprive events of their contingency. History thereby becomes the *parousia* of *Geist* (Hegel), the story of liberty (Croce), the triumphant march of the essential ideals that constitute the American experience, etc. History is that which is written so that the past will not be known; or will be known only insofar as it finds fruition in the future. Traumatic events that would enervate the national consciousness—Hiroshima for example—are justified by explanations invented after the fact. History is the narrative written retrospectively to wash the blood from our hands. And as such it is a discourse whereby a collective ego-identity is forged through the banishment of nagging doubts and fears—a melodramatic allegory play, rife with resentment, whereby a collectivity triumphs over time and contingency. Plays that offer resolution and "catharsis" perform a similar function by creating structures of feeling that cleanse the psyche by bathing it in the pleasure and release provided by secondary emotions. Aristotle's famous distinction between poetry and history misses the main point. Within the system of guarantees history and drama are *fictions* that perform the same function in different ways. As the two arts dedicated to the exorcism of existential contingency, they give the metaphysical need that informs the ratio with a "local habitation and a name." That name is *Humanism*: the set of essentialistic beliefs about human nature that we use to assure our transcendence of historical, existential, and psychological contingency.

Drama is the agon that erupts whenever those guarantees are shattered. One then exists in the knowledge that conflict is the essence of being human not the temporary departure from the essence. Psyche is its conflicts; nothing within protects us from the need to *act* and through action to submit ourselves to a world that estranges us forever from the paradise of the guarantees. Humanism is that wing of the ratio that is of most concern to us because it is the application of the ratio to our psyche and our experience. Once we have internalized the humanistic *ethos,* conflict can only be experienced as the movement **from** and **to** the recovery of an identity that we cannot lose, an identity fitted with the added benefit of assuring our goodness, our psychological health, and our correspondence with fundamental, unalterable values. Such is the experience that theatre within the system of guarantees offers its audience. It does so by violating the essential thing that theatre incarnates. *Representation exceeds intention.* Any halfway decent play engages conflicts that exceed the guarantees. Unfortunately, the latter then far too often come to impose themselves upon the emerging drama so that it can end—as every play of Arthur Miller's does—with the re-assertion of every belief the play has thrown into question. Playwriting within the orbit of the guarantees is the clash of contradictory imperatives. This is so not because we are faint-hearted in the face of experience, but because the traditional forms and principles of dramatic structure are the aesthetic realization of the guarantees. The pull toward resolution embodied in traditional dramatic forms is one with the underlying ideological and emotional guarantees that are thereby satisfied. Genuine experimentation and newness in the theatre thus begins only when we write and perform in ways that *deracinate* all conventions and artistic principles that wed us to the guarantees. Arthur Miller argues that "every drama is a jurisprudence." The law of drama however is not the translation of abstract thought into temporal terms. It is the submission of guarantees to their reversal and the liberation of what emerges when experience is represented cleansed of their intrusion.

10.

Against catharsis. Historical explanation within the system of humanist guarantees and catharsis within the emotional dynamics of form are two different ways of fulfilling the same metaphysical need. Aristotle was Plato's apt pupil in one regard. He knew that the disruptive power of drama had to be contained. What better way than to impose secondary emotions (pity and fear) upon it and then argue that the *logos* of dramatic structure was the movement of those emotions to their purgation. He thereby invented Tragedy in order to banish the tragic. The limit of theatre is the limit of our will to explore agons that will not be bound by the need to produce catharsis. But to get there we have to become aware of all the ways in which we remain bound to that desire; as, for example, in messianic aesthetics and the belief in the redemptive power of art. To know history we must experience our situation without deriving succor from the aura that the desire for redemption casts over it.

Against irony. But to achieve our goal we must overcome something that is for many of us far more binding than the guarantees. We must overcome our misplaced confidence in the postmodern exaltation of irony and the "death of the subject" as the last word in liberation. A theatre of free play sounds experimental and historically liberating only if one forgets that the last word on irony was pronounced long before the aporias of the self-ironizing sensibility began to strut and fret their hour across the stage of culture in an effort to conceal an underlying despair.

> "Irony. Don't let yourself be controlled by it, especially during uncreative moments. When you are fully creative, try to use it, as one more way to take hold of life. Used purely, it too is pure, and one needn't be ashamed of it; but if you feel yourself becoming too familiar with it; if you are afraid of this growing familiarity, then turn to great and serious objects, in front of which it becomes small and helpless. Search into the depths of Things: there, irony never descends." (Rilke, *Letters to a Young Poet*)

Nor does the cant offered by a slew of ideologues that 9-11 marks the end of post-modernism and the return to "reason and moral clarity." What we need, in opposition both to dogmatic deconstructionism and moral posturing, is to press on and constitute what has long slumbered in the post-modern condition as its true contribution to our historical awareness—the supersession of irony by the tragic and with it the recovery of a genuinely existential way of thinking about concrete experience.

Incipit Tragoedia. For it is in a frank opening of ourselves to despair that we find our way back into an authentic relationship with the grave and serious things, a way to live in the temporality of the fundamental questions not as prisoners of nostalgia but in the confidence that such a relationship alone gives us the courage to once again explore agons that derive from the depth of human inwardness. Being a subject will then become again what it was for Hamlet—not an illusion to be deconstructed in the deferral and delay of endless signification ("signifying nothing") but the agon in which "the human heart in conflict with itself" (Faulkner) endures the existentializing claims that tragic experience makes upon us: "for I have heard/That guilty creatures sitting at a play/ Have by the very cunning of the scene/Been struck so to the soul, that presently/They have proclaim'd their malefactions." (*Hamlet* II.ii.588-92). Our task is to do everything in our power to make that happen.

11.

Drama has a unique cognitive and ontological status. Freud said "the tragic poets knew it [the unconscious] first." We can now see that they also know it best; know it in a way that goes beyond the limits of other ways of knowing. Authentic drama is that representation of concrete, lived experience that comprehends what happens when we are delivered over to ourselves. In destroying those structures of feeling that protect us from ourselves, drama opens the psyche to an order of self-mediation that becomes possible only when traumatic conflicts are sustained in agons equal to them. As C.S. Peirce said "experience is what happens when our ways of knowing break down." Drama is that happening. It is what breaks within us when all ideological blinders, all rationalistic guarantees, are submitted to an agon in which we exist as at issue and at risk in the struggle to mediate the burden of primary experiences. The proper relationship between the image and the order of the concept is thereby established. The world of the image, of concrete experience, is our way of apprehending realities that exceed the limitations of the concept. The cognitive power of literature subject Plato's argument banishing the poets to a complete reversal. "Poets are the unacknowledged legislators" in a world that reason knows little of, a world in which traumatic images are sustained in agons that prove equal to a representation of experience engaged at a level that is visceral, primary, and existentially exacting. Literature is not the translation of abstract concepts and themes into temporal, narrative terms; it is the world as it is lived existentially in structures that are prior to reason and beyond its range of comprehension.

12.

Here is a task for a dramaturg of the future. We don't need censorship, we have interpretation. The history of dramatic criticism from Aristotle to the present is a monument to the effort to superimpose the guarantees upon drama by constructing theories and interpretations that take the tragic, explorative energy of great works and bend them to our needs. Thus Aristotle: offering us the catharsis of emotions that are themselves a defense against the tragic. Milton: "calm of mind/all passion spent" so that we can leave the theatre assured that nothing will change. And in our time, the many varieties of ritual theatre (Burke, Girard, Frye, etc.) that turn drama into a group psychology in which social conflicts are transcended through the imposition on experience of patterns that are held to be universal and a-historical. By and large the history of dramatic criticism constitutes so many conceptual shields before the Medusa, ways of letting us get close enough so that we can slay what we can't look upon directly. What we need is a dramaturg who will reverse that tradition by exposing all the ways that the guarantees are sequestered in interpretations. We need a method of interpretation that will prepare the way for radically new productions through concrete demonstrations of how great works undermine the interpretations that have been foisted upon them. Scholarly research would then itself become a drama of *a-lethia*, of wresting from concealment. We'd thereby learn, for example, that virtually everything that has been written on *Hamlet* constitutes an attempt to avoid the play. Despite different frameworks of meaning, the interpreters of *Hamlet* share an identical goal: to turn the most radically open-ended and emergent exploration of the tragic in our literature into something cabined, cribbed, confined in the narrow house of our needs and desires.

13.

And of course we need a theatre of the oppressed, a theatre that will be feminist and gay and multi-cultural, for these are the places where the contradictions of our historical situation are most apparent. We need a theatre that honors every subject-position. But in liberating such voices our purpose cannot be the celebration of diversity as an end in itself. For we live in one world—now more than ever. And so our task remains *dialectical*—to apprehend the contradictions that define the social order as a whole and thereby discover the necessary connections that bind us to a common task. No subject position can be excluded from this search for we can never know when the contradictions of the whole won't become apparent and assault our psyche in a way that tears our world to tatters: as in the eyes of JonBenét Ramsey and what they reveal about our most cherished institution, the American family.

And of course we need a theatre that is grandly experimental. But all experiments must derive from a single rationale: to shrink the space between us and the audience to that the audience is forced to become a participant in the performance. Thus I envision a theatre in which every device is exploited to make actors and audience inseparable. As when, for example, the actors, with the play in some way already begun, would form a queue the audience must join and move along in order to get to their seats; or when at points during the performance the lights would go up in the house so that audience members would become painfully aware of one another; or when perhaps they would at intermission find the doors of the theatre locked and a discussion of the work already begun among the cast and actors planted in the audience, a discussion they would be invited to join. What has become one of the most deleterious conventions of recent theatre—the post-play discussion—would thereby become the itch of an anxiety felt at the time it should be. We have only begun to explore all the ways we can break the fourth wall through experiments that will be disciplined because they serve a single end: to activate an agon in the audience. That is the purpose of playing, the concern that informs everything we do from the moment we first begin to write or read a play and search for ways to activate the most radical of encounters.

14.

Here, then, in summary is an ideal realization of the action that a great drama performs on the audience. (1) Social identity is maintained through the public, legitimation rituals through which shared ideologies are celebrated. Drama reverses that process by exposing those rituals: by blocking their function and turning them back against themselves. (2) As group psychology the agon thereby engaged has the following structure. The audience, as group, tries to resolve conflict by coalescing around a shared need (laughter, pity etc) which offers a collective identity. The ensemble's task is to destabilize this structure. Defenses must be activated; the sores of discontent rubbed raw; projections turned back against themselves. (3) The collective psyche then regresses to a more primitive state in an attempt to ward off deeper underlying conflicts. With the fragmentation of group identity each individual is delivered over to the drama of primary emotions. As in *King Lear* "close pent up guilts" break loose in an audience confronted with the return of buried conflicts. (4) The miracle has happened: an audience has been transformed from a group seeking pleasure through the discharge of tensions and the affirmation of common values to anxious agents existentialized in a solitude that has arisen, in the midst of others, as the space of a fundamental concern. Tragic recognitions ensue, destroying the possibility of regaining the psychological identities that existed prior to the play. (5) The audience now experiences in the characters on the stage the fundamental truth: that what we don't know about ourselves is what we do—to the other. They experience it in sufferance as the imperative to deracinate everything that hides one from oneself.

(6) The purpose of authentic drama is to destroy the ego in order to awaken the psyche. The ego cringes in the theatre because it witnesses the staging of its informing motive. Flight from inner

conflict is its reason for being. (7) Our job is to reverse that process; to represent an audience to themselves so that they will, in the shock of recognition, see and suffer what they want to deny. Thereby the smooth functioning of secondary emotions gives way to an agon of primary emotions in subjects who now find themselves in fundamental conflict with themselves. (8) Once that has happened, the task of the ensemble is to bring that audience to the recognition that there is only one choice: radical change or the extinction of consciousness; persistence in inner paralysis and the deadening of affect or the effort to reverse oneself totally through the struggle to overcome everything that protects one from confronting one's deepest conflicts.

(9) Theatre has become a place of total exposure, with no "catharsis" available to relieve the audience of the burden that has descended upon it. Aristotle was right in this—reversal and recognition are the essence of tragedy. They are what happens to the audience when they prove equal to the agon that a great play activates within them. When that happens the space of theatre has been totally transformed. The audience isn't looking at the play. The play is looking at them with a look that has the Sartrean power to expose us to our bad faith and reestablish our contact with our existence. (10) The purpose of theatre is to awaken this possibility and bar all exits that would deliver us from it. Theatre is not the space in which a content—a body of themes or preexisting ideas—is communicated. It is the space in which an action is performed. That action is the attempt to act on the psyche of the audience in order to bring about a reversal in the relationship that they live to themselves.

15.

"Always historicize." A trauma cannot be resolved until it has been constituted. That is why one cannot write a play that will resolve the trauma of 9-11, for example, without being untrue both to drama and to history. Which doesn't mean we won't be deluged with plays and productions dedicated to healing the national psyche. That has, after all, been the national mandate since 9-11. As such it reveals the persistence of the root assumption we must deracinate: the assumption that trauma is only resolved through the restoration of guarantees; concretely, in this case, through dramas of pathos followed by a triumphant reaffirmation of the a-historical ideals that constitute "the American character" and America's unique role in history. Therein lies the ideological formula for pseudo-drama: our innocence, our unexampled suffering, our triumphant recovery. Any representation of 9-11 that does not serve this structure is forbidden. And so here, as prologue to a drama that will not exist, I offer these "fragments shored against" our "ruins"—a primer toward the recovery of what the *image* reveals about history and our collective unconscious.

Image is the native language of the psyche, the language in which the truth of history and the impact of history upon the psyche is expressed in a logic which, like the logic of the dream, establishes hidden and unexpected connections in which the present speaks to and reawakens the past in the re-emergence of everything that ideological consciousness strives to deny. *Ground-zero.* What's in a name? The term now used to designate the rubble of what was once the World Trade Center was the term coined in Alamogordo, New Mexico to identify the epicenter where the first Atomic Bomb was detonated. It was then used to locate the same place in Hiroshima and Nagasaki so that we could measure with precision the force of the Bomb and gauge its effects. Through a grotesque and cunning reversal it now designates what was done to us. But in doing so it also reveals an unwritten history. Hiroshima, a repressed memory deep in the American psyche, returned on 9-11 as we experienced in diminished form what it must have been like to be in Hiroshima city on August 6, 1945 when in an instant an entire city disappeared abandoning the *hibakusha*, the walking dead, to a landscape become nightmare. For us, however, repressed memory only returns to serve the defense mechanisms of *projection* and *denial*. The term Ground-zero thus offers no entry into our past; instead, it gives us a new identity as the innocent victims of a terror we have the temerity to claim is unprecedented and that we demand the whole world acknowledge as such. In doing so we reveal our relationship to history. History is hagiography, the assertion of our virtue through our triumph over the forces of evil. From which follows the parade of heroic images whereby we rise phoenix-like from the ashes, united as a Nation that has recovered its essence and thus goes forth to reaffirm the ideals it represents by undertaking the actions needed to cleanse the world of terror. John Wayne lives—and he's been called upon once again to provide the American imaginary with the images it needs to deliver it from images of another order.

For the images blazed into our consciousness on 9-11 are terrifying precisely because they embody anxieties that open up the psychotic register of the psyche. A plane embedded surrealistically in a building; bodies falling from the sky; that great granite elevator going down; the black cloud rushing forth to engulf a fleeing multitude; and then the countless dead, buried alive, passing in endless queue across the shattered landscape of the nation's consciousness. The dark dream of psychosis—of falling endlessly, going to pieces, collapsing in on oneself, losing all orientation, being delivered over to a claustrophobic world of inescapable, ceaseless suffering—found in 9-11 the objective correlative that awakened images buried deep in the national psyche; images of things forgotten, ungrieved, vigorously denied.

For a historical consciousness incapable of agon, however, the only operation traumatic images permit is *evacuation*. And so, for the media and those comfortably seated in the places of ideological power, the projector had already started running and on the screen of the national psyche flashed old, familiar images of a movie full of patriotic sentiment and patriotic gore. Flags a-bursting, the heroic dead of ground-zero are resurrected in the acts of war we undertake in their name, their image blending and fading into the images of our triumphant military action in Afghanistan, in Iraq, in North Korea, in any place we designate a haven of "terrorism," that term the blank check on which we draw to do whatever it takes to restore us the way we were restored by the incineration of Hiroshima and Nagasaki. And restored we were as witnessed by another image from the past that flares up here to confirm what Walter Benjamin defines as the mission of the dialectical historian: "Every image of the past that is not recognized by the present as one of its own concerns threatens to disappear irretrievably." Navy Day, October, 1945, a crowd of 120,000 gather in the Los Angeles Coliseum to celebrate a simulated reenactment of the Bombing of Hiroshima, complete with a mushroom cloud that rises from the fifty yard line to the joyful cheers of that rapt throng. The first Super-Bowl: the new American collectivity as it gains orgasmic release in hymn of praise to the burgeoning cloud that ushers in its hour upon the stage of human history, a collectivity in Hosanna before the image of its inhumanity as it blossom before them, big with the future.

Einstein said "the Bomb changed everything except the way we think." It didn't change that because no drama was written with the power to implode/explode the *fact* of that Event in the psyche so that the Bomb would be internalized as a crisis for the soul and not just another fact to justify, before capping that justification with the claim that the one nation that used the Bomb has the moral right to determine who should have it.

And so the parade of images that echo and exorcise other images creeps on apace. As after Gulf Storm, the Nintendo war, a war represented on TV as a video game. No images of the 100,000 Iraqui dead were permitted entry into the national conscience; nor subsequently any images of the million Iraqui civilians that have now died as a result of our sanctions. (Yes, Saddam bears a lion's share of the blame. So do we!) Instead with victory the proclamation of George H. Bush—"we've finally put an end to Vietnam syndrome"—and so can safely confine that war and its vast body of traumatic images to oblivion and the dust-bin of history. We thus repeat over time the same Pyrrhic victory—a victory over those traumatic images that call the psyche to a knowledge of itself. Which is why such images can only return from without as violent and unwarranted assaults on the "innocence" of a people who refuse to know their actual position in the world.

Five percent of the world's population consume 25 percent of its resources—and they do so by exerting control over the destiny of other countries. But that fact finds no image in our consciousness. And in Rio de Janeiro, at the one ecological conference he attended, George H. Bush delivered a proclamation even more chilling than his crowing about Vietnam syndrome: "The American way of life is not negotiable. "As long as that dogma remains in place, there will be many more *ground-zeroes*.

And so for some of us traumatic images remain the weight that weighs like a nightmare on the brains of the living. A drama that would be adequate to 9-11 would resolve nothing. It would, instead, deliver the audience over to a history that would reveal the historical, dialectical connection of the pattern of images presented in this section in order to awaken that audience from its collective slumber. For those of us who work in the theatre, Walter Benjamin's great aphorism about the task of culture—"the dead remain in danger"—must be emended thus: the dead remain in danger—of being sacrificed to the needs of the audience.

16.

The previous sections have offered fifteen ways of making a single, complex point. All are different and all are necessary. For they are dialectically connected. It is in that dialectic that theatre finds its rationale and its mode of being. Our first job and our last is to cast the audience. But the only way to do so is by first casting ourselves in a way that deracinates within ourselves everything that stands in the way of the most radical act—the engaging of primary emotions in mediations that remain true to the agon that primary emotions activate within us. For the ability to perform such an action on an audience is only given to those who first perform that action in themselves.

17.

All our efforts depend on a single circumstance. Kafka at 24 offered this as the task of reading/writing.

"If the book we are reading does not wake us, as with a fist hammering on our skull, why then do we read it? Good God, we would also be happy if we had no books, and such books as make us happy we could, if need be, write ourselves. But what we must have are those books which come upon us like ill-fortune, and distress us deeply, like the death of one we love better than ourselves, like suicide. A book must be an ice-axe to break the sea frozen inside us."

We will get the kind of plays we need only when we have become the kind of audience who come to the theatre demanding plays that perform such an action within us.

ENDNOTES TO THERE IS ANOTHER COURT

Because the essay is written for a general audience I have confined discussion of a number of scholarly and theoretical issues to Endnotes.

1. For the most complete analysis of the autopsy, see Cyril H. Wecht and Charles Bosworth, Jr. *Who Killed JonBenét Ramsey: A Leading Forensic Expert Uncovers the Shocking Facts.* (Signet/New American Library, 1998). For analysis of the autopsy by those experts who advised the Boulder Grand Jury, see Lawrence Schiller, *Perfect Murder, Perfect Town* (Harper Collins, 1999), pp.43-46, 361-362, 436-437 and Steve Thomas, *JonBenét: Inside the Ramsey Murder Investigation* (St. Martin's Press, 2000), p.253.
2. This editorial was written by James R.Gaines, former Managing Editor of *Time.*
3. The testimony of housekeepers indicate that bedwetting (and other matters of cleanliness) were of relative unimportance to the Ramseys. See Schiller, p.237, 560-561.
4. Smit presented his theory of the case on a Katie Couric Special Hour-Long Interview on NBC in 2001. For Smit's views see also Schiller, pp.268-269. This theory has always had and continues to have a number of supporters in the Boulder D.A.'s office, many of whom have also expressed their view that no parent could commit such a grisly crime.

One suspects we have not seen the last in the political and legal machinations that have characterized this case from the beginning. See note #5 for a development that occurred just as this book was about to go to press.

5. It is not my purpose to review the evidence that has been gathered in support of the two theories nor to evaluate that evidence. A number of books already exist on this topic. It should be pointed out, however, that a preponderance of evidence supports the view that the murder was an inside job. The intruder theory, always a creature of precarious conjectures, has not withstood scrutiny. All the "evidence" adduced to support it either cannot be tested (the stun-gun) or has been explained in a way that offers no support to the intruder hypothesis. On the murder as an inside job, see Schiller, pp. 235,368, 386-388 and Thomas, pp. 241-244, 254-255, 346-347, and Wecht, *passim*. On the intruder theory, see Schiller, pp. 575-576 and Thomas, pp. 323-324, 346-347.

A word is needed here, however, regarding the latest development in the Ramsey affair. Judge Julie Carnes of Atlanta, the Antonin Scalia of U.S. District Court Judges, used the occcasion of dismissing a libel suit against the Ramseys by Chris Wolf to give her opinion on a far weightier matter: namely, that in her view there is no evidence showing the parents killed JonBenet and considerable evidence indicating that an intruder did it. See *Wolf v. Ramsey. Westlaw citation: 2003WL1821525 (N.D. Ga)*. The primary basis of the judge's reasoning appears to be this piece of sophistry: Steve Thomas had no previous experience with murder cases before heading the Ramsey investigation while Lou Smit is "an expert investigator who has successfully cracked other child murder investigations." The bastion of weak rhetoric—the argument from authority—is thus invoked to obviate the need for rigorous scrutiny of the complete body of evidence that exists in support of the two theories. Which did not stop Judge Carnes from indulging her own version of Catch-22: namely, that to win his libel case Chris Wolf would have had to put the Ramseys on trial for murder. Emboldened by Carnes' example of judicial reasoning, Boulder District Attorney Mary Kennan within a week of the ruling issued a statement expressing her agreement with the judge's views. Before doing so Kennan clearly did not review her own police files since as former Ramsey Special Prosecutor Michael Kane pointed out in a recent T.V. appearance (*The Abrams Report, MSNBC, July 18, 2003*) there is in those files ample evidence contradicting the misleading data on which Judge Carnes based her opinions. Kennan's statement capped an involvement in the case distinguished by opposition to police investigators and favoritism to the Ramseys. For example, Ms. Kennan, under the threat by the Ramsey's attorney of a suit against the city of Boulder, met with the Ramseys in private for 4 hours in February of 2003, at which time she also took the case out of the hands of the Boulder police. Judge Carnes, incidentally, excoriates the police for releasing information to the media but makes nary a mention of the far greater number of anti police leaks from the Boulder D.A's office. (See Schiller, *passim*, Thomas, *passim* and Wecht, pp.333-335.)

In light of such considerations, it is worth noting that the judge's ruling abounds in errors of fact and interpretation. The latter occur when a debatable conclusion is drawn with no consideration given to other ways the data can be interpreted and, more importantly, no recognition given of the non-evidentiary and non-scientific status of what is cited as "undisputed evidence" permitting only one inference. To cite just a few examples. In commenting on the rope and cord found at the crime scene, the judge claims that the defendants did not possess such items. What she apparently doesn't know is that we will never know what the Ramseys possessed because John Ramsey's whereabouts for an hour after the arrival of the police the morning of the crime are unaccounted for and because Patsy's sister Pam was permitted to remove several boxes of items from the house in the days immediately following the crime. (See Thomas, pp. 56-58.) And so *vide* the duct tape the judge claims the Ramseys didn't possess. *Vide* her claim that a rope found in a brown paper sack in the guest bedroom did not belong to either defendant; though here, significantly, the only basis for the judge's conclusions appears to be the defendant's claim that the rope wasn't theirs. Other errors stem from the judge's ignorance of the rudimentary knowledge about the case available to anyone who takes the trouble to read a book such as Lawrence Schiller's *Perfect Murder, Perfect Town*. For example, the judge cites the complex knots in the rope and cords fashioning the garotte and claims that neither defendant possessed the knowledge required to make them. Apparently she is unaware that John Ramsey was in the U.S. Navy and owned a boat which the whole family enjoyed. Equally troubling is the judge's cavalier citation as "undisputed evidence" indicating an intruder of facts—such as the "HI-TEC" brand shoeprint found in the basement, the suitcase near a window, etc—that are susceptible to a number of other explanations, some of which derive from the very situation she acknowledges in criticizing police investigators; namely, the contamination of the crime scene by John Ramsey, Fleet White, and police investigators. *Vide* the reference to the unidentified DNA found in JonBenet's panties and the single male pubic hair found on the blanket covering her; though here what Judge Carnes apparently doesn't know is that a number of innocent explanations are possible for such data and, additionally, that those explanations are backed by known facts. (See Thomas, pp.153-154). Most troubling of all is her references to the stun-gun as "undisputed evidence" of an intruder since the original proponent of the stun-gun theory, Lou Smit, acknowledges that the only way to prove the theory is by exhuming the body of the deceased.

But hypothetical reasoning in terms of the method of multiple working hypothesis (on which see below, section number 8) is not the judge's forte. She typifies, in contrast, a particularly egregious example of the fallacy of precarious selectivity: in the collection of data, its interpretation, and, most pointedly, in excluding the mass of evidence undermining the hypothesis that has a hypnotic hold over her attention. The wealth of evidence that points to Patsy is reduced to a single consideration—whether Patsy wrote the ransom note. That question is then decided on the basis of favoring one panel of experts and excluding the testing of others, both those made available by the plaintiff and those cited in Schiller. Another alarming sign of single-mindedness concerns those "facts" from which the judge derives a significance totally at odds with the view of all experts. For example, she cites approvingly the profile of the killer published by the Ramseys in their book (and earlier, unbeknownst to the judge, in a newspaper ad). The judge describes this profile—"a male ex-convict, aged 25-35, who is familiar with and owns a stun-gun"—as "detailed" unaware, apparently, that former F.B.I. profiler Gregg McCrary judged it superficial and useless due to its vagueness and generality. Another kind of naivete marks the one reference the judge makes to the *content* of the ransom note—the instruction to John Ramsey

AN EVENING WITH JONBENÉT RAMSEY 185

that he "use that good southern [sic] common sense"—as evidence Patsy didn't write the note since she knows John is from Michigan. The possible sarcasm of the reference and its consistency with the phraseology of a southern Belle such as Patsy escapes the judge. As does something far more important, which as a jurisprude the judge should know. When in court a lawyer opens an issue it must then be pursued rigorously wherever it leads. With respect to the content of the ransom note, that principle should have led the judge to a consideration of the detailed and often brilliant examination by Andrew G. Hodges in *A Mother Gone Bad* (Village House Publishers, 1998) of the ransom note in terms of its similarity in phraseology, content, the use of acronyms, etc. to other documents written by Patsy Ramsey. Such perceptions would, however, have led the judge in directions she was unwilling or unable to pursue. In this connection it is worth noting the judge's concurrence with the view of Lou Smit and most members of the Boulder D.A.'s office that the grisly nature of the murder argues against a mother's involvement. That belief, an *idee fixe* which has an *a priori* status for proponents of the intruder theory, flies in the face of the knowledge established by the F.B.I. that only 1 in 12 child murders is committed by someone outside the family and that the details of such murders are often, indeed, grisly. Incidentally, Judge Carnes sees no evidence of "sexual abuse" in the Ramsey family history yet cites as evidence of an intruder Lou Smit's statement that the deceased was a "pedophile's dream come true."

All of the peculiarities of Judge Carnes' ruling are traceable to a single circumstance. Judge Carnes' knowledge of the "Ramsey case" in general is restricted to what was presented to her in a civil libel proceeding. That is, (1) to Chris Wolf's repetition of the weakest parts in Steve Thomas' accidental-murder-due-to-bed-wetting scenario and Wolf's representation by an attorney, Darnay Hoffman, who was unable to gain access to police files and thus was in no position to counter when the Ramsey's attorney, Lin Wood, exploited the situation in order to enter, as undisputed "evidence", matters that correct knowledge would have easily refused. A similar absence of adequate information underlies Judge Carnes' acceptance of Wolf's presentation of the evidence pointing to Patsy as the murderer as a complete rendering of the evidence against Patsy when it is, in fact, no such thing. The larger body of evidence pointing to Patsy was never heard in Judge Carnes' court. She remains sublimely unaware of what is known by anyone who has done the basic reading on the case. Given what was presented to her, the dismissal of Wolf's libel claim is understandable. What isn't is the presumption by Judge Carnes to opine on matters regarding which she lacks both the requisite knowledge and authority.

But I'm toiling in pitch. For what comes across most clearly in the judge's prose is the virtual scripting of her ruling by Lin Wood. Indeed, the ruling reads like a brief written by the Ramsey's legal team. The ruling is littered with non-sequiturs, all pro Ramsey. For example, "nothing out-of-the-ordinary occurred at the party [the Ramseys went to on the evening of the murder] and the Ramsey family appeared happy," the implication being that this constitutes evidence neither parent could have gone home and committed murder when, of course, it signifies nothing save our common ability to don the masks that social occasions require. Similarly, the litany of misleading claims by the Ramseys to have cooperated fully with investigators is repeated by Judge Carnes as an unquestioned article of faith. The Ramsey's suggestions regarding suspects who should be investigated are also repeated without acknowledging that over 100 suspects were investigated and cleared by the police. Moreover, given the judge's excoriation of the police, the unmistakable implication is that those suspects she names remain so. This is especially sad and needlessly cruel in the case of the cleared and now deceased Bill McReynolds ("Santa") and his widow. (See Carnes, p.30). But then the Ramseys have shown a careless disregard for who they name as suspects (a list that includes a number of formerly close friends) along with a keen appreciation of the advantage of continuing to defame said suspects long after the Ramseys know that their "suspicions" are false. The real scandal, however, is that a judge would use the limited situation of a libel case to advance broad and sweeping statements on the Ramsey case in general, knowing, as she must have, that those statements would take on in the media a status disproportionate to her knowledge and at odds with the vast body of evidence she would have been forced to look at were she presiding at a criminal trial conducted by a competent prosecutor. In this, of course, she played into the hands of Lin Wood who from the beginning has done O.J.'s lawyers one better, Wood's general strategy being through press conferences to use the media to influence and intimidate the Boulder D.A.'s office in order to prevent there ever being a trial.

It is often asked what lasting damage Scalia and "the felonious four" (former prosecutor Vincent Bugliosi's term) did to the legal system in pulling off the judicial *coup d'etat* that put an end to a democratic, electoral process because, in Scalia's immortal reasoning, letting the vote count continue would have done grave harm to Mr. Bush's legitimation. In Judge Carnes' ruling we have a stunning instance of the kind of fallout we can expect from the High Court's example. Judicial nullification before the fact on behalf of the privileged—a demonstration of how easily legal firepower can bend the law to its designs. Not suprisingly, the Ramseys hailed the ruling as full vindication (Lin Wood: "essentially this was a civil murder trial") and it was reported as such in a media eager to give the quietus to JonBenet so that it could turn its attention to "fresh woods and pastures new."

6. Dan Rather *48 Hours Special,* CBS, 1998. On the purchase of the videos by the networks and the awareness of the "sex angle" as the key to selling this story, see Schiller, pp. 68-69.

7. Schiller, pp.68-71.

8. In the wake of the Ramsey case, no serious public discussion about child beauty pageants, the sexualization of children by their parents and the tacit assumption that parents have a right to use their children in such ways took place. Nor, to my knowledge, has there been any effort to advance the idea that Social Services should investigate such families, to say nothing of the possibility of introducing legislation to criminalize such activities. Nor, as number 1 indicates, has there been any effort by local authorities and agencies to stem the growth of a budding industry— the child beauty pageant.

Psychoanalytic discussion of the case has, of course, been eschewed by the media. With one noteworthy exception—the tabloids. Here it thrives because it is rendered ridiculous and perverse—the free invention of sick minds. The tabloids thus fulfill their ideological function—to discredit psychoanalytic thinking by presenting its parody.

9. Rainer Maria Rilke, "The Fourth Duino Elegy," *Ahead of All Parting: The Selected Poetry and Prose of Rainer Maria Rilke* (edited and translated by Stephen Mitchell) (Random House, 1995).

10. See Schiller, p. 556 for the comments of Linda Wilcox who worked as a Ramsey housekeeper. The data collected here is derived primarily from Schiller's book, *passim*.
11. The medical records of Dr. Beuf, the Ramsey's pediatrician, show that between the age of 3 and her death JonBenét made over twenty-five visits to the doctor's office. Primary complaints: persistent cough, poor sleep, diarrhea, bad breath, congestion, vaginitis, loss of appetite, bladder infection with vaginal discharge, possible blood in stool. Throughout this period Doctor Beuf was also aware of JonBenét's continued bed-wetting. As statements in interviews with Diane Sawyer and with KUSA-TV indicate, Doctor Beuf saw none of this as out of the ordinary. It should also be noted that Doctor Beuf is a close family friend who was among those who sat with the Ramseys on December 26, 1996. It is perhaps also worth noting that on December 17, 1996 Patsy Ramsey placed three phone calls to the doctor's office. No explanation of the reason for these calls has been tendered. See Schiller, pp. 255-258.
12. On the concept of psychosexual identity, see Walter A. Davis *Inwardness and Existence: Subjectivity In/And Hegel, Heidegger, Marx, and Freud* (U of Wisconsin P, 1989), pp. 296-313.
13. For a disingenuous discussion of this topic see John and Patsy Ramsey, *The Death of Innocence* (Thomas Nelson Publishers, 2000), p. 53 where they attribute JonBenét's success in the pageants to her "gusto and infectious smile." JonBenét, indeed, had these gifts but they were not the talents that she was encouraged to develop by her mother, her grandmother, and the coaches procured to prepare her to perform in the pageants. See Schiller, pp.93-95.
14. See the classic essay by Joan Riviere, "Womanliness as Masquerade," *International Journal of Psychoanalysis*, X, 1929, pp. 303-313.
15. F. Scott Fitzgerald, *The Great Gatsby* (Collier Macmillan, 1992) p.21.
16. Jean-Paul Sartre, *Being and Nothingness* (Philosophical Library, 1956). See especially, pp.89-95, 255-265, 286-291.
17. This paragraph applies Hegel's seminal insights into master-slave psychology to the mothers behind the pageants.
18. On this concept of the goal of theatre, see Antonin Artaud, *Selected Writings* (California, 1988), pp. 215-267.
19. In the suppression of that way of understanding and being, the media

does for common culture what postmodernist dogmas do for high culture. Their combined working manifests the central contradiction of our time. The voiding of the psyche and the death of affect. The attainment of closure at any cost or its simple inversion: i.e., the belief that the only healthy response to painful realities is one that rids the psyche of all "negative" feelings or the perpetual deferral of closure as the way of keeping reality confined in a purely conceptual space. There is no subject. No master narrative. No reference. Nothing but the play of socially constructed discourses in the uncontrollable proliferation of texts (media events) producing more texts in an endless self-cancelling commentary on one another, proof perfect of the "vertiginous possibilities of linguistic aberration" (Paul deMan) and the impossiblity of arresting this or bringing it to anything but *aporia*. Irony as enlightment—paralysis turned into an achievement. And so everything is "always already" delivered over to the endless play of dueling experts and the redoubtable wisdom of Dr. Henry Lee: "they will have two experts to counter your one expert and that is why you must have three." The texts thus pile up—Schiller's interviews of 194 people resulted in 25,000 pages of transcript; Thomas' investigation included 590 interviews, consultation with 64 outside experts, the clearing of over 100 possible suspects and a case file of 30,000 pages—spinning ever further away from the traumatic center which cannot be seen or known. The moment we open our mouths she vanishes. Language is always on holiday. The more we talk, the more intently, the more we generate what is finally mere noise. This wisdom is now the law and the prophets and thanks to the media the morn and evening prayer of the postmodern subject.

20. This has been the dominant post-structuralist theory of the subject and of human identity. Representative formulations include Ludwig Wittgenstein, *Philosophical Investigations* (Macmillan, 1958), Jacques Lacan, *Ecrits: A Selection* (Norton,1977), Jacques Derrida, *Of Grammatology* (Johns Hopkins UP,1974) and Paul deMan, *Allegories of Reading* (Yale UP, 1979).

21. Reader response criticism comes in many flavors. They all have one thing in common—an attempt to protect the reader from the threat posed by the literary work. Norman Holland thus develops a psychoanalytic theory based on the defenses of the ego and the need to assert them whenever a

literary work creates anxiety. Wayne Booth and the Chicago critics discuss emotional response in terms of the need of writers to assure their audiences that their beliefs and values will not be undermined by the literary work. Stanley Fish in his inimitable way trumps everyone by arguing that a literary work is no more than the interests that diverse literary communities impose upon it. A literary work is whatever we want it to be and our reason for making it so is a function of arbitrary self-interest controlled by the career imperative. For a representative sample of reader response approaches, see Jane Tompkins, *Reader Response Criticism* (Johns Hopkins UP, 1980). One way to look at this moment in criticism: reading is dangerous, texts psychologically disruptive, and so ways had to be found to protect the reader and the professional literary institution from that which has the power to challenge the former and expose the latter.

22. For example, Smit makes much of the fact that unidentified DNA was found in JonBenét's panties. This sounds significant. Unless one knows that there are innumerable innocent ways that DNA could have gotten there. Moreoever, the DNA cannot be dated and thus has no evidentiary significance. On this see Thomas, p.298-299 and Schiller, p.576.

23. This is the concoction of Detective Ainsworth. See Schiller, p.407. While any flight of fancy is possible, it is also possible to call fact itself into question. In this the plum goes to one Dr. Richard Krugman who countered the testimony of a number of experts on the sexual abuse of JonBenét thus: "I don't believe it's possible to tell whether any child is sexually abused based on physical findings alone." See Schiller, p. 361.

24. Once investigators started to follow the Ramsey's prompting there was no way they could refuse to follow whatever "lead" the Ramseys decided to provide, including Patsy's suggestion that every male student at the University of Colorado with a bicycle should be considered a suspect. More distressingly, the Ramseys have regularly fingered some of their (former) closest friends as suspects who should be investigated.

25. Bobbie Rosencrans, *The Last Secret: Daughters Sexually Abused By Mothers* (Safer Society Press, 1997).

26. Schiller, p.583. It is interesting that Schiller removes this paragraph from the paperback version of his book.

27. Schiller, p.584.

28. It is not my purpose here to discuss the many limits that the inherent

positivism of the legal system imposes on what can count as truth in a Court of Law. Nor to show how pervasively ideological factors (1) inform the legal-juridical determination of knowlege, (2) marginalize disciplines such as psychoanalysis and feminism, and (3) construct the "subject" of judicial action in ways that reflect dominant social prejudices. A number of studies can now be cited in support of a single conclusion. The law is not a disinterested court of rationality determining truth by objective, value-free, neutral, purely scientific criteria. It is yet another institution in which social relations of power determine knowledge for ideological reasons. Along with the pioneering work of Michel Foucault on this subject, see David S. Caudill and Stephen Jay Gold (eds.) *Radical Philosophy of Law* (Humanities Press, 1995), Peter Goodrich, *Oedipus Lex: Psychoanalysis, History, Law* (U of California P, 1995) and Alan Hyde, *Bodies of Law* (Harvard UP, 1996).

In terms of our subject, the main conclusion that can be drawn from all of this is a salutary reminder. What a study of the law teaches is how little we can know within the framework of the law. The ideological implications of that recognition are profound because the hegemony of the legal-juridical determination of what is real and the subjection of subjects to this way of thinking is the primary ideological development of our time. With disastrous consequences. For when the legal-juridical becomes the way that the general public thinks about all questions we will have alienated ourselves from some of our most vital and significant ways of knowing. The movement toward such a situation is now well advanced; and the discourses that have been developed about the Ramseys provide a revealing example. The main function of the media today is to train us to think along legal-juridical lines and to regard other ways of thinking as subjective and thus private, unverifiable, and ineffable. In Foucaultian terms, to be a subject today is to be subjected to a discourse in which everything stands under legal surveillance. What counts as real and as fact is what can be constituted as evidence in a court of law. That is all there is; all that is the case. Everything else is subjective and lacks any "truth claim." Qua subject one is what can be said legally about one. What happened is what can be constituted forensically by scientifically recognized experts. And thus most of what we know, especially when we dare to think along psychoanalytic lines, is deprived of any standing *a priori.* Once we tailor ourselves to the terms of the law we have lost contact with lived experience and all it reveals. The overriding ideological agenda will thereby come to fruition: we will no longer be able to experience our own experience except in legal-juridical terms.

29. The most informative, up to date website on the Ramsey case is : *www.acandyrose.com.* There were at one time over 150 sites devoted to the crime, most taken up with the kind of thing one would expect. Amateur sleuths out to amaze one another with their discovery of the "fact" everyone else has overlooked and how it is the key to solving the crime.

30. Thomas' tale falls naturally into the genre of idealistic young man fighting a corrupt system. Smit's becomes the sentimental narration in which a wise old man dispenses the wisdom of years to a younger, less studious generation. Such narratives signal the death of the noir genre where the detective succeeds not only because he is willing to see the darkest realities in his subject but because he is open to the darkness in himself.

Schiller's book presents the fascinating example of how the pull of one genre counteracts the claims of another. Schiller's intention is to write a book that will be a monument to the objective gathering of data and its sifting in terms of legal-juridical considerations. That investigation builds to the grand conclusion that no explanation can be formulated that handles all the data. What Schiller actually presents, however, is an inadvertent parody of "objectivity" within a hilarious social comedy of Boulder as a community. Schiller's personae is that of the pure observer collecting all the "data," even if only for the benefit of future studies. The trouble is that for Schiller evidence is anything anyone says about anything. Furthermore, because "objectivity" makes it impossible for him to scrutinize what he is told, every statement is given the status of "evidence" in a cornucopia of contradictory assertions that cancel out one another. To give one example, which bears directly on the hypothesis I've advanced. On the question of sexual abuse Schiller presents as countervailing evidence the testimony of the Ramsey's pediatrician assuring him that his records indicate nothing out of the ordinary. Armed with that assurance Schiller sees no need to reflect on the close personal relationship of the good Doctor to the Ramseys nor to submit the Doctor's medical records to the scrutiny of those experts who could have assured him that something is definitely awry here. It would be nice to say that what we have in Schiller is a bundle of "data" in search of a hypothesis but that would imply methods of interrogation foreign to Schiller's hyperempiricism. There is, however, a *felix culpa* at work here as one "witness" after another reveals their naivete or their venality to the most credulous of reporters. As a result everything stands revealed: the Ramsey's neighbors eager in the effort to outdo one another in proclaiming the goodness of the community and their "knowledge" that good people like John and Patsy could not have done anything amiss; the hollowness of the Church, its consolations, and the skill of the Ramseys in exploiting this connection; the bungling efforts of police investigators and the obfuscatory politics of the District Attorney's office as one rube after another comes up with a "big idea" which is countered by the bright child of another careerist intent on advancement. Schiller can't capitalize on the comic potential of any of his materials, however, because he is wedded to his own curious impersonation of Joe Friday (I'm just trying to get a story though for the life of me I have no idea what the story is). When one has no story to tell, no narrative framework, one doesn't achieve objectivity; one achieves Babel.

31. James Joyce would have loved the Ramsey's book. American self-fashioning—the commodified signs one clothes oneself in to give oneself a socially acceptable identity. As an exercise in such activity the book is in its way a classic, its beauty lying in its excess. The Ramseys don't know where to stop. They must make themselves the representatives of every virtue, the defenders of every value. In the course of the book they become the defenders of the Constitution, waging a heroic battle against the threats to our liberties posed by the police and the media. The representatives of Family Values in a cold and impersonal world. (As Patsy informed us in her first public appearance on the *Larry King Show*, "America is suffering because it has lost faith in the American family.") The spokepersons for Christianity called on to witness how their deep commitment to Christian values enabled them to endure their ordeal. In the Ramseys the narcissistic needs of the individual and the spirit of capitalism are wedded: one must always be annexing yet another value, the superfluity of one's march through ideological hyperspace a perfect match to the inner void that informs it.

A further charm of all this is the recognition that the Ramsey's book was written, in effect, by a committee of lawyers and media consultants. As such the book is a definitive example of ideology in its pure state, virtually free of context; ideology as the set of empty commonplaces that can be enlisted on behalf of anything. Spin doctoring at its finest. Nixon vivant. We've seldom been given as clear a glimpse into the laboratory of cynical reason. Team Ramsey (Steve Thomas' term for the group of legal and media experts gathered about the Ramseys) knows the truth about contemporary America. Everything is image, a play of hollow and empty signs that can be manipulated to put the desired spin on anything. Perhaps the greatest lesson that shines through in all of this is the hollowness of the languages the Ramseys invoke. In claiming every humanistic commonplace for themselves they reveal how empty of content the language of humanism has become, how today it is little more than a collection of empty platitudes ready to serve any occasion, the staple of politicians and presidents eager to deceive. The truth of the Ramseys' book is that it contaminates everything it touches because what Freud said of the hysteric is true of its authors: they ooze betrayal. The characteristic human ability to delude oneself here becomes a monument to mendacity. The abstract moralism of their language constantly calls attention to its subtext. In this regard perhaps the most noteworthy thing about the book is the relative absence of JonBenét in it. Every time the Ramseys try to talk about her they draw a blank, the language becomes an abstract claim about their love followed by heavy doses of the Hallmark sensibility. JonBenét never emerges as more than the projection of their needs. In life and in death. Like every other human gesture, genuine mourning is beyond the Ramseys. It has to be; otherwise it would interfere with their overweening need: to defend themselves from every possible charge by claiming for themselves every possible virtue. On all this see especially the pages devoted to JonBenét and child beauty pageants, pp.50-60.

32. See, for example, Robert C. Solomon, *The Passions* (Notre Dame P, 1983) and Richard Wollheim, *On the Emotions* (Yale UP, 1999).

33. The book I'm currently writing develops a theory of primary emotions and their significance for a theory of subjectivity and human identity. The effort of the book is to synthesize existential and psychoanalytic ways of thinking in a theory that will preserve the traumatic dimensions

of subjectivity in what may be termed, with a bow to Hegel, a phenomenology of tragic spirit.

34. Walter A. Davis, *Deracination: Historicity, Hiroshima, and the Tragic Imperative* (SUNY P, 2000). One main strand of this book is an examination of the assumptions that constitute the *ratio* and the limits they place on our understanding of history. The essential gesture of Reason is the effort to transform everything into concepts, into moral and quasi-theological ideas, in order to assert as the being of the human subject a rational identity that is freed of desire and inner conflict. Once this self-conception is in place it provides the guarantees that enable one to contain the disruptiveness of any event or phenomenon.

35. See, for example, Judith Herman, *Trauma and Recovery* (Basic Books, 1992), Cathy Carruth (ed) *Trauma* (Johns Hopkins UP, 1995), and Lenore Terr, *Too Scared to Cry* (Harper and Row, 1990). One general assumption in such works is that while traumatic experience is beyond language it is healed when it is articulated in the language of therapy to a sympathetic listener. There is, of course, a hidden circularity in such views. And something more distressing: traumatic experience is deprived of its inherent intelligiblity. The only meaning it can have is conferred on it from outside.

36. Walter A. Davis "Death's Dream Kingdom: The American Psyche After 9-11," *Journal for the Psychoanalysis of Culture and Society*, volume 8, number 1, pp.127-132.

37. The best articulation of this position is provided by Wayne C. Booth in a number of books. See especially, *The Company We Keep* (U of California P,1988) and *The Rhetoric of Fiction* (U of Chicago P,1961).

38. In *Get the Guests: Psychoanalysis, Modern American Drama, and the Audience* (U of Wisconsin P, 1994) I challenge such theories by showing how great plays concretely expose and destroy the defenses of the audience. They experience they thereby make possible is one of knowing what we don't want to know about ourselves and our world.

39. Alice Sebold, *The Lovely Bones* (Little, Brown and Company, 2002).

40. Daniel Mendelsohn, "Novel of the Year," *The New York Review of Books*, vol. L, number 1 (Jan. 16, 2003), pp.4-8.

41. Most theories of ideology focus primarily on ideas, beliefs, and ideational commonplaces. They thereby leave out of examination the foundation of

the entire edifice. That foundation is in the feelings that underlie and give force to other ideological determinations. Too often ideology is pictured solely in terms of how ideas and commonplaces—America is a beacon of democratic ideals; Capitalism is the system that corresponds to human nature; etc.—control how subjects think about their world. But such ideas click—and stay in force regardless of evidence to the contrary—because of the feelings they serve. The primary result of ideology in America is that the ego of the average American experiences the need to maintain certain feelings (happiness, optimism, pride) and to banish anything that interferes with or is contrary to those feelings. With such a formation in place the possibility of serious thought about traumatic events is rendered impossible. And so certain ideas and beliefs persist despite strong evidence to the contrary because certain feelings are peremptory. They cannot be corrected because one's identity depends upon them. They are more important than any consideration. Truth and reality always bend to their demands. It is these feelings and nothing else that determines what goes on under the guise of thinking and reasoning. For example, X is upset by a play and therefore concludes that the play is a bad work. X then supports that opinion with the theory that good works must produce catharsis. That argument makes sense because it derives from the prior feelings that it protects and defends. The study of ideology is the attempt to remove the rationalizations that prevent us from seeing and combating such processes. Its ultimate subject accordingly is what I call a *feeling formation*; i.e., the determination of a subject's emotional responses so that one way of feeling is made necessary and other ways proscribed.

42. Is there an audience for tragic representations? That is the question since, as we've seen, the tragic is a fundamental challenge to ideology, the ego, secondary emotions, and all our prevailing myths, especially about the family. We laud its counterfeit, melodrama, but we stay as far as possible from the real thing. Perhaps a work is tragic in the extent to which it is resisted and attacked by the audience. For the tragic is an invitation to internalize what we can know only insofar as we suffer it independent of guarantees and the closure they assure. A work is tragic insofar as it refuses to adapt itself to the needs of the audience. A tragic work does not manipulate suffering for our benefit; it offers suffering to us as our highest

possibility. That is why, from a tragic perspective, virtually everything that has been written and said about tragedy, especially humanistic statements made in praise of it, is heavy with resentment and resistance.

43. For this view, labeled by its author psychoanalytic, see, Jessica Benjamin *The Bonds of Love* (Random House, 1988). According to Benjamin's theory parents have the magical ability to bracket their psyches while they perform their necessary social function in transmitting the "bonds of love" that assure their children of an ego identity that is strong, stable, and normal. (Ideologically all of this is, of course, a perfect fit with what the American family wants to believe about itself.) Given what we now know about the instances of sexual and psychological abuse of children within the family, Benjamin's claim to be offering a psychoanalytic theory of the origins of the subject is one of the more telling instances of how far American psychoanalysis has departed from its subject. Benjamin's mentor, Daniel Stern, in *The First Relationship* (Harvard UP, 1977) and *The Interpersonal World of the Infant* (Basic Books, 1985) is a central figure because his theorizing attempts to account for the origin and the development of the "self" and of human identity. The self in Stern, however, is essentially a product of the adaptation of cognitive abilities to social, normalizing processes. In keeping with the assumptions that rule ego psychology, identity can only be conceived as the development of socially normalizing beliefs and behaviors. It is impossible within such assumptions to make or retain any meaningful contact with the actual life of subjectivity and the conflicts that define the psyche. As Freud showed, *psyche* begins on the other side of the processes Stern describes. It is what happens, for example, when experiences such as humiliation, shame, envy, and love create a being who recognizes itself as utterly and existentially at risk in its relationship to the other. Psyche as subject is the living out of the relationship one has to oneself as a result of the conflicts that derive from such experiences. The life of the psyche has nothing to do with development toward normalizing relationships and cognitive, adaptational abilities. That such a view has become the dominant way of conceiving identity and the self in American "psychoanalysis" is a sign of the sea-change initiated by Heinz Hartmann's attempt to focus psychoanalysis in America on the ego, its defenses, and the process of adaptation. In the developments that Hartmann's thought founded

everything disruptive, challenging, and inherently tragic in Freud was sacrificed to the effort to make psychoanalysis a respected and functioning member of capitalist society. Lacan provides the most insightful psychoanalytic critique of the ego. See especially, *Ecrits* and *The Seminar of Jacques Lacan, Book Two* (Norton, 1991). Russell Jacoby *Social Amnesia* (Beacon, 1975) and Philip Cushman *Constructing the Self, Constructing America: A Cultural History of Psychotherapy* (Perseus, 1995) provide the corresponding ideological critique. Psychoanalytic ego psychology (and its more recent offspring in self, object-relations, and relational psychoanalysis) is a perfect fit with capitalist ideology because it gives one a way to talk about oneself by investing in a language that measures identity by how well one has adapted to the imperatives of the social structure. The proof comes with the ability to convince oneself that one's identity as a self lies in the incessant iteration of affirmative commonplaces about oneself and one's world. Self here is not a lived experience of a depth within oneself defined by one's relationship to the conflicts that cause one anxiety. It's a discourse one practices in order to give oneself the sense that one has achieved identity in a conflict-free ego sphere that has triumphantly vanquished all nagging doubts and fears.

44. Placing that issue once again in a psychoanalytic and tragic context could have been the value of JonBenét for feminism. Though she presents a striking case of the sexualization of women as objects, she has been for the most part neglected by feminist scholars and writers, probably as an example out of step with the tune of the time. Consider, for example, two examples that bear on the question of theatrical representation—Eve Ensler's *The Vagina Monologues* and the theorizing of Drucilla Cornell. There are traumatic episodes in Ensler's play, some of deep tragic resonance, but trauma is contained with an ideological and Utopian celebration of feminine sexuality. That sexuality is invoked in an almost incantatory way to encourage the audience to share in proclaiming the healing powers of an experience that a large proportion of those in the audience can claim only by engaging, and now in a highly public way, in an old and debilitating game—faking an experience one hasn't had in order to fulfill the demands of the other. In this case the big Other of feminism in its celebratory phase. A similar ideological insulation from the conflicts of actual experience characterize Drucilla Cornell's Derridean assurance—in

a statement formulating the program of much contemporary feminist performance art—that theatre offers women the route to a new identity through the "playful performance" of a "choreographic text with polysexual signatures." See, Drucilla Cornell, *The Imaginary Domain: Abortion, Pornography, and Sexual Harassment* (Routledge, 1995). Such freedom is a far cry from the actual agons of actual women and would, for example, have been airy nothing to one such as JonBenét who, had she lived, would have faced a tragic situation that would permit only one agon as adequate to what was done to her: "My sexual being was taken from me. The scars of the other rule whenever I am touched. I must reclaim my sexuality or destroy myself in the process." Both Ensler and Cornell are unable to sustain contact with the conflicts central to such a problematic of psychosexual identity. As a result Ensler finds in the Utopia of the few the model imposed on the many; Cornell in linguistic play the illusion that one can fashion an identity for oneself through a free play devoid of psychological insight and concrete struggle.

45. See *Inwardness and Existence*, pp.232-313.
46. Steven Pinker, *How the Mind Works* (Norton, 1997), pp456-460. See also, pp. 370-375, and 446-449.
47. A philosophic understanding of the tragic would apprehend the distinct contribution made by tragic poets from Aeschylus through (say) Faulkner to a single understanding of the fundamental structures of tragic experience. Such a knowledge would constitute a history formulating the essential insight that each seminal tragic work makes to an evolving understanding that knits all into an overarching world-view. Tragic knowledge would thereby attain what, in Hegelian terms, would be its notional identity: a comprehension of the origins, immediacies, and fundamental contexts of experience as tragic process. In effect, one would construct for the tragic an analytic of experience analogous to the analytic of *Dasein* that Heidegger develops in *Being and Time*; i.e., a fundamental ontology of the tragic contexts that define the human condition.

APPENDIX

In order to assure prospective theatres that the play *Cowboy's Sweetheart* is on sound legal ground, I submitted the work to a First Amendment lawyer, Devin Schindler. He read the play, had legal research done on the issues raised by the work, and provided me with the following Memorandum.

FACTS

Walter Davis, a professor at Ohio State University, wrote *JonBenét, the Musical* [retitled *Cowboy's Sweetheart*]. This play is based on the JonBenét Ramsey murder case and intertwines the history of the case with other materials in an artistic effort to illustrate the author's ideas and interpretations of present day society and its judicial system.

ISSUES

I. Are members of the Ramsey family public figures who must show by clear and convincing evidence that a person against whom they have claimed libel made false statements with actual malice?

II. Has the author of an artistic *docudrama* that is based on his creative interpretations of a true story reached an element of actual malice by including uncertain truths?

SHORT ANSWER

The Ramseys are limited-purpose public figures, and therefore must have clear and convincing evidence that Professor Walter Davis made false statements against them with actual malice. Because Professor Davis' artistic work constitutes a *docudrama*, he is permitted to make creative alterations of fact regarding the murder of JonBenét. To the extent the "facts" portrayed in the play are based on information obtained from reliable sources, and Professor Davis has not knowingly disregarded the truth, the play is not actionable because there could be no showing of "malice."

DISCUSSION

"Limited-purpose public figures" are individuals who voluntarily inject themselves into a particular public controversy, thereby making themselves public figures for a limited range of issues. 50 Am. Jur. 2d *Libel and Slander* no. 74(1995). For any public figure to prevail in a libel claim, that figure must establish that the declarant of the alleged liable knew the statements being made to be false or acted in reckless disregard for the truth, rather than just "simple negligence." 50 Am. Jur. 2d *Libel and Slander* no. 31 (1995); see also *Mason v. New Yorker Magazine, Inc.*, 501 U.S. 496, 510 (1991).

I. The Ramsey's are Limited-Purpose Public Figures

To determine whether an individual is a limited-purpose public figure, courts use various tests. One test adopted by several Circuits of the Court of Appeals requires the following: (1) the controversy at issue must be public in the sense that people are discussing it and people other than immediate participants will feel the impact of its resolution; (2) plaintiff claiming libel must have more than a trivial role in the controversy; and (3) the alleged defamation must be germane to the plaintiff's participation in the controversy. *See* 50 Am. Jur. 2d *Libel and Slander* no. 75 (1995). A second test to determine whether a plaintiff is a limited-purpose public figure requires the defendant to establish that plaintiff has: (1) successfully invited public attention to his or her views in an effort to influence others; (2) voluntarily injected self into public controversy; (3) assumed a position of prominence in the public controversy; and(4) maintained regular and continuing access to the media. *See* 50 Am. Jur. 2d *Libel and Slander* no. 75 (1995); *Foretich v. Capital Cities/ABC,* 37 F. 3d 1541, 1553 (4*th* Cir. 1994) (summarizing these tests as determining "whether the plaintiff 'voluntarily assumed a role of special prominence in a public controversy in order to influence its outcome'" in relation to Supreme Court cases involving the issue of limited-purpose figures.) Because both tests have similar requirements with the second being more involved, for efficiency purposes, analysis will focus on the second test.

The District Court of Colorado determined that the murder case and events surrounding the death of JonBenét Ramsey constitute a legitimate public interest. *Miles v. Ramsey & National Enquirer, Inc.,* 31 F. Supp. 2d 869, 875 (D. Colo. 1998). Davis' play therefore involves a matter of public concern, meeting the requirement as set forth by both tests.

In determining whether the Ramseys "voluntarily assumed a role of prominence in a public controversy in order to influence its outcome," under the final three steps of the test, it is necessary to look at the actions taken by the Ramseys. Unlike the plaintiff in *Foretich*, the Ramseys did "freely choose to publicize issues," did discuss the matter in question with the press, did not limit involvement to that necessary to defend themselves, and did draw attention to themselves in order to invite public comment or influence the public, "seek[ing] to arouse public sentiment in [their] favor." *Foretich*, 37 F. ed at 1555-57 (holding that plaintiffs were not public figures because they did not *voluntarily* inject themselves into the public controversy). On march 17, 2000, John and Patsy Ramsey published **The Death of Innocence**, a book in which the Ramseys offer their own recollection and theories of what happened the night JonBenét was murdered. MSNBC New Services (June28,2001),*at*http://www/msnbc.com/Modules/

RamseyTimeline/031700.asp In their book, the Ramseys name who they believe are possible suspects in the murder of their daughter, including names not suggested by police. The Ramseys **voluntarily** published this book, drawing attention to themselves in order to influence the public. The publication was not a "reasonable" response like that found in *Foretich*, because the Ramseys' response was excessively published and not proportionate. *Id.* At 1563.

These circumstances are analogous to those presented in *Reuber v. Food Chemical News*, where the court held that the plaintiff was a limited-purpose public figure, because he voluntarily injected himself into a public controversy by authoring and disseminating a study which challenged the government's conclusions regarding the controversy at issue. *See Reuber v. Food Chemical News, Inc*, 925 F.2d 703, 710 (4th Cir. 1991). In this case, the Ramseys similarly authored a book that challenged the conclusions and opinions of the government, represented by the police, in efforts to influence the public.

Because the Ramseys voluntarily injected themselves into the public controversy surrounding the case of JonBenét's murder both by publishing their book and constantly being in the forefront of the media, they reach the status of limited-purpose public figures. *See* 50 Am. Jur. 2d *Libel and Slander* no. 73 (1995) (stating that an individual is a limited-purpose public figure if one injects oneself into a particular public controversy.

II. The First Amendment allows for a modicum of Creative License in Theatrical Productions Based on Actual Events.

A. *The Standard For Holding Authors of "Docudramas" about Public Figures Liable is Very High.*

In order for the Ramseys, as limited-purpose public figures to pursue a valid libel claim against Davis for the publication and production of his play, "clear and convincing evidence" must demonstrate that Davis' artistic creation was written and published with actual malice. *See* Am. Jur. 2d *Libel and Slander* no. 34 (1995),

Street v. NBC, 645 F. 2d. 1227, 1236 (6th Cir. 1981), *cert. granted*, 454 U.S. 815, *cert dismissed*, 454 U.S. 1095 (1981) (citing Supreme Court case *Gertz v. Robert Welch, Inc.*, 418 U.S. 323, stating that a "plaintiff [alleging libel] may not recover under the malice standard unless there is 'clear and convincing proof' that the defamation was published 'with knowledge of its falsity or reckless disregard for the truth'"). Courts define actual malice as *knowledge* that the information was false or a *reckless disregard* of whether it was false or not. See *Davis v. Costa-Gavras*, 654 F. Supp. 653, 654 (S.D.N.Y. 1987) (citing Supreme Court case *New York Times v. Sullivan*, 376 U.S. 254 (1964), defining "actual malice").

The Supreme Court requires that the inquiry of actual malice focus on the publisher's state of mind. See *Davis*, 654 F. Supp. At 656 (citing Supreme Court case *Monitor Patriot Co. v. Roy*, 401 U.S. 265 (1971) (holding that a public figure plaintiff failed to present evidence that filmmakers intentionally portrayed a defamatory suggestion against her with knowledge or doubts of its truth). *Davis* is a libel case brought by a public figure regarding a film based on a true story in which she was involved. *Id.* At 659. Many courts interpret the Supreme Court's "actual malice" requirement to mean that a public figure claiming libel must have evidence that a "publisher actually entertained serious doubts about the veracity of the publication, or that there are obvious reasons to doubt the veracity of the informant or the accuracy of his reports." *Davis* 654 at 656. "There must be clear and convincing provable evidence that defendants *knowingly* and *falsely* published the alleged defamation of the film, or in fact entertained *serious doubts* as to the truth of the films alleged defamatory statement." *Id.* at 656.

Courts have determined that "when the truth is uncertain and seems undiscoverable through further investigation, reliance on . . . [reliable] sources is not unreasonable." *Street*, 645 F. 2d at 1237 (holding various findings of a judge and doctor in a trial as reliable sources on which a publisher could rely upon). Because reliable, credible tabloids held the Ramseys as possible suspects, and the truth to the events surrounding JonBenét's murder has been uncertain and undiscoverable, Davis reasonably relied on such sources. Although, the Ramseys have sued these media outlets for libel on the behalf of Burke [their son, officially cleared by police investigators], many cases are still pending, and thus an uncertainty as to the truth of events still exists.

B. *A Play is a Docudrama, a Creative Interpretation Not Claiming Absolute Truth*

Authors of fictionalized accounts of actual events involving public figures can exercise a modicum of creative license without losing their first amendment protections. Courts have distinguished documentaries from *docudramas*. A documentary is a "non-fictional story or series of historical events portrayed in their actual location; a film of real people and real events as they occur." A docudrama is a "dramatization of an historical event or lives of real people, using actors or actresses . . . a docudrama partakes of author's license—it is a creative interpretation of reality—and if alterations of fact in scenes portrayed are not made with serious doubts of truth of the essence of the telescoped composite, such scenes do not ground a charge of actual malice." *Davis,* 654 F. Supp at 658 (holding that a docudrama is a "minor fictionalization [and] cannot be considered evidence or support for the requirement of actual malice," and dismissing the complaint because plaintiff provided no evidence that defendants knew their interpretations were false.)

Davis' play is clearly a docudrama. Actors and actresses are used to portray the real people to help the author illuminate his creative interpretation of events. Professor Davis admits that his artistic creation of *JonBenét the Musical* (retitled *Cowboy's Sweetheart*) is a work of fiction. He is also allowed to suggest that the play is his belief of the events that transpired, or his creative interpretation of reality.

The Ramseys may attempt to argue that Davis portrays events with actual malice or recklessness, because he interprets facts and events differently than they do. As Davis and his script mentions, however, the play displays Davis' views of present society and its judicial system. As stated by the court in *Street*:

An individual's social philosophy and political leanings color his historical perspective. His political opinions cause him to draw different lessons from history and to see historical events and facts in a different light. He believes the historical evidence he wants to believe and casts aside other evidence to the contrary. So long as there is no evidence of bad faith or conscious or extreme disregard of the truth, the speaker in such a situation does not violate the malice standard. *Street,* 645 F. 2d at 1237.

In *Street,* plaintiff claimed libel against NBC and alleged that NBC's play, or docudrama, portrayed her in a derogatory light. The court held that there was no actual malice and that a playwright has the liberty to leave out certain facts, while adopting others, as long as he or she does not demonstrate extreme disregard of the truth. *Id.* at 1273. A plaintiff cannot rely solely on the fact that a publisher sees history and events in "a different light" to show evidence of "actual malice."

Furthermore, a publisher of a docudrama has the liberty to alter facts and recreate conversations from memories. In *Davis,* the court dismissed a claim brought by a public figure that claimed libel against those associated with the creation of a docudrama in which plaintiff was portrayed. The court found that there was no actual malice because the film was a docudrama and not a documentary, and thus the author had the liberty to make alterations of facts as long as they were not made with serious doubts of truth. *Davis,* 654 F. Supp. At 658 (stating also "In docudrama, minor fictionalization cannot be considered evidence or support for the requirement of actual malice"). The court in *Masson v. New Yorker Magazine, Inc.* determined that because docudramas are historical fictions, quotations of characters in docudramas should not be interpreted as actual statements of speakers. *Masson v. New Yorker Magazine, Inc.,* 501 U.S. 496, 513 (1991).

Reliable tabloids, such as the New York Post and Time, have suggested that JonBenét's parents had something to do with her murder and sexual abuse. Walter Davis' creation of a docudrama based on the events surround JonBenét's murder does not suggest bad faith or extreme disregard of the truth, because Davis reasonably relies upon credible publications for his facts. Davis' production instead displays a non-actionable "creative interpretation of realit[ies]."

ABOUT THE AUTHOR

Walter A. Davis, Professor Emeritus at The Ohio State University, is the author of a number of books of cultural criticism including *Inwardness and Existence, Get the Guests, and Deracination.*

0-595-76468-1

Printed in the United States
32295LVS00007BD/2